Y0-CDJ-305

**New Directions for
Adult and Continuing
Education**

Susan Imel
Jovita M. Ross-Gordon
COEDITORS-IN-CHIEF

Linking Adults with Community: Promoting Civic Engagement through Community Based Learning

Susan C. Reed
Catherine Marienau
EDITORS

Property of Library
Cape Fear Community College
Wilmington, NC

Number 118 • Summer 2008

Jossey-Bass
San Francisco

LINKING ADULTS WITH COMMUNITY: PROMOTING CIVIC ENGAGEMENT
THROUGH COMMUNITY BASED LEARNING
Susan C. Reed, Catherine Marienau (eds.)
New Directions for Adult and Continuing Education, no. 118
Susan Imel, Jovita M. Ross-Gordon, Coeditors-in-Chief

© 2008 Wiley Periodicals, Inc., A Wiley Company. All rights reserved. No part of this publication may be reproduced, stored in a retrieval system, or transmitted in any form or by any means, electronic, mechanical, photocopying, recording, scanning, or otherwise, except as permitted under Section 107 or 108 of the 1976 United States Copyright Act, without either the prior written permission of the Publisher or authorization through payment of the appropriate per-copy fee to the Copyright Clearance Center, 222 Rosewood Drive, Danvers, MA 01923, (978) 750-8400, fax (978) 646-8600. The copyright notice appearing at the bottom of the first page of an article in this journal indicates the copyright holder's consent that copies may be made for personal or internal use, or for personal or internal use of specific clients, on the condition that the copier pay for copying beyond that permitted by law. This consent does not extend to other kinds of copying, such as copying for distribution, for advertising or promotional purposes, for creating collective works, or for resale. Such permission requests and other permission inquiries should be addressed to the Permissions Department, c/o John Wiley & Sons, Inc., 111 River Street, Hoboken, NJ 07030; (201) 748-6011, fax (201) 748-6008, www.wiley.com/go/permissions.

Microfilm copies of issues and articles are available in 16mm and 35mm, as well as microfiche in 105mm, through University Microfilms Inc., 300 North Zeeb Road, Ann Arbor, Michigan 48106-1346.

NEW DIRECTIONS FOR ADULT AND CONTINUING EDUCATION (ISSN 1052-2891, electronic ISSN 1536-0717) is part of The Jossey-Bass Higher and Adult Education Series and is published quarterly by Wiley Subscription Services, Inc., A Wiley Company, at Jossey-Bass, 989 Market Street, San Francisco, California 94103-1741. Periodicals Postage Paid at San Francisco, California, and at additional mailing offices. POSTMASTER: Send address changes to New Directions for Adult and Continuing Education, Jossey-Bass, 989 Market Street, San Francisco, California 94103-1741.

New Directions for Adult and Continuing Education is indexed in CIJE: Current Index to Journals in Education (ERIC); Contents Pages in Education (T&F); ERIC Database (Education Resources Information Center; Higher Education Abstracts (Claremont Graduate University); and Sociological Abstracts (CSA/CIG).

SUBSCRIPTIONS cost $85.00 for individuals and $209.00 for institutions, agencies, and libraries.

EDITORIAL CORRESPONDENCE should be sent to the Coeditors-in-Chief, Susan Imel, ERIC/ACVE, 1900 Kenny Road, Columbus, Ohio 43210-1090, e-mail: imel.l@osu.edu; or Jovita M. Ross-Gordon, Southwest Texas State University, EAPS Dept., 601 University Drive, San Marcos, TX 78666.

Cover photograph by Jack Hollingsworth@Photodisc

www.josseybass.com

CONTENTS

EDITORS' NOTES

Adults are increasingly called upon to become involved in the body politic in order to strengthen their communities, promote change, and enliven our democracy. Competing with the call for civic engagement is the fact that adults are overcome by "busyness" (Daloz, Keen, Keen, and Parks, 1996) as they meet increasing demands from their workplaces, provide a wealth of opportunities for their children, and meet the caregiving needs of their parents and others. Twenty-nine percent of individuals find the time to volunteer in their churches, schools, and parks (U.S. Bureau of Labor Statistics, 2005). Yet the need for active civic engagement is urgent, according to Art Chickering, whose chapter (Chapter Eight) makes a plea for service opportunities that will promote a more sophisticated analytical ability among all of us as adults and lift our culture from dualistic perspectives that tend to drive our social policies.

Service learning is a form of experiential learning in which universities and community based organizations and nonprofits partner to promote the growth and development of both students and community residents. Widely used with both high school and traditional-age college students, this methodology has been credited with a range of outcomes, including greater reflective abilities, personal growth, and the likelihood of volunteering after college. Community colleges and universities serving undergraduate and graduate adults increasingly utilize service learning in a way that accounts for the practical and developmental needs of adult students and adults in the community.

Through service learning or community-based learning, adults participate in the kind of experiential learning that engages cognitive, affective, and conative dimensions of learning as they confront complex issues and concepts within the context of human lives. Adult learning scholars are examining how this engaged approach to learning contributes to deeper learning and to the individual growth and development of adult learners. This methodology offers adult learners the opportunity to interact with others whose community, race, or class differs from their own. These interactions often lead to the questioning of one's assumptions and shifts in perspectives, including perceptions of self and others. And, adults may make connections within their own communities that lead to more active civic engagement. Ultimately, community based projects can potentially enhance learning, facilitate civic engagement, foster partnerships between academy and community, and promote social change.

The design of community based learning projects is crucial to the accomplishment of these laudatory outcomes as has been discussed in

the service learning literature for years. Adding the unique challenges and opportunities of employing this methodology with adults requires an analysis of the adult learning literature as well as identification of practices that will be effective with adults. This volume will bridge these two bodies of literature in order to articulate best practices and illustrate their implementation.

M. Cecil Smith begins the volume by reviewing the service learning and adult development literature to show how the two bodies of knowledge can contribute to each other and to identify important areas of future inquiry. Next, Barbara Holland and Gail Robinson set a broad context for community based learning that includes an overview of efforts to involve adults in community based learning in higher education, the workplace, and the community.

The next three chapters highlight specific projects and programs that involved adult learners in community based learning. In Chapter Three, Rachael Richter-Hauk and Julie Arias provide an example of how a partnership that emphasizes structured reflection can contribute to the development of professional values for social work students. In Chapter Four, Liz Largent and Jon Horinek share the results of a formative evaluation of their service-learning program's first year, which indicated that adult students were less satisfied than younger students. Analysis of these data informed programmatic changes that were implemented in the second year. A different context for community based learning is presented by Karsten Mündel and Daniel Schugarensky in Chapter Five, where they discuss learning among volunteers in community organizations in Canada and explore how intentional reflection could enhance adult and organizational development.

The next two chapters address key elements of community based learning, influenced by distinctive characteristics of adult learners that can be applied to various kinds of community based learning offerings. In Chapter Six, drawing on the literature in adult learning and service learning, Catherine Marienau and Susan Reed identify important choices that educators will need to make as they design community based learning courses for adults. Primary attention is given to who adults are as learners and educators' perspectives on teaching and learning. Next, Morris Fiddler and Catherine Marienau highlight the essential role of reflection in learning by using a model of "learning from events" that can enhance adults' ability to derive meaning from experience.

In Chapter Eight, Art Chickering assesses the necessity for adult engagement and finds a "crying need" in our society. Like Smith in Chapter One, Chickering sees promise in the adult development literature that community based learning promotes commitment to civic engagement and raises the bar for robust research in this area. In the final chapter, Chapter Nine, Reed and Marienau respond to Chickering's call to action by analyzing the role that community based learning could play in sustaining lifelong commitment among adults. Together the authors in this volume explore the hope, challenge, and possibilities of linking adults to communities to promote their own learning as well as the learning and welfare of others.

New Directions for Adult and Continuing Education • DOI: 10.1002/ace

The reader will note that the terms "service learning" and "community based learning" are used throughout the volume. "Service learning" is more commonly used to refer to "a form of experiential education in which students engage in activities that address human and community needs together with structured opportunities intentionally designed to promote student learning and development" (Jacoby, 1996, p.5). We use the term "community based learning" to refer more broadly to learning derived from community based work conducted either by volunteers or students in higher education. There is some debate in the literature about which term best reflects the reciprocity and equality in campus-community relations that proponents of both terms consider important.

Susan C. Reed
Catherine Marienau
Editors

References

Daloz, L. A., Keen, C. H., Keen, J. P., and Parks, S. D. *Common Fire: Lives of Commitment in a Complex World.* Boston: Beacon Press, 1996.

Jacoby, B., and Associates. *Service Learning in Higher Education: Concepts and Practices.* San Francisco: Jossey-Bass, 1996.

U.S. Bureau of Labor Statistics. *Volunteering in the US, 2005.* 05–2278 www.bls.gov/newsrelease/volun.nr0.htm

SUSAN C. REED *is associate professor in the School for New Learning, DePaul University, where she employs community based learning to teach about access to health care.*

CATHERINE MARIENAU, Ph.D., *is professor and faculty mentor in the School for New Learning, DePaul University, where she works with adult undergraduate and graduate students.*

1

Within the context of adult development, theories are highlighted that suggest research on the impact of service learning on adults.

Does Service Learning Promote Adult Development? Theoretical Perspectives and Directions for Research

M. Cecil Smith

Service learning is one of the most pervasive education innovations of the past generation and has demonstrated much success in connecting schooling with community service. Service learning is designed to be integrated into, and enhance, the academic curriculum. It is believed, and there is growing evidence to show, that participation in service learning can foster civic responsibility on the part of children, youth, and college students. Also, a number of investigations have shown positive academic benefits for child, youth, and college service learning participants. In fact, participation in service learning as part of a college course has been found to have more positive benefits for students than does participating in typical volunteer community service (Vogelgesang and Astin, 2000).

But what about those nontraditional college students who are older adult learners? Does participation in service learning afford any benefits to these individuals, in terms of greater community participation, altruism, academic performance and skill development, personal growth, or leadership ability? A definitive answer to this question is not yet available because there are few investigations of service learning that have involved older, nontraditional adult students or other adults. Generally, adults tend to be the recipients of, rather than participants in, service learning. Fenzel, Peyrot, Speck, and Gugerty (2003), however, surveyed nearly three hundred alumni of one college and found both behavioral and attitudinal differences between those adults who had participated in course-related service learning and those

NEW DIRECTIONS FOR ADULT AND CONTINUING EDUCATION, no. 118, Summer 2008 © 2008 Wiley Periodicals, Inc.
Published online in Wiley InterScience (www.interscience.wiley.com) • DOI: 10.1002/ace.291

who had been volunteers while in college. Service learning participants were more likely to have been recently involved in community service in the period after completion of college, compared to the alumni who had performed volunteer activities. Service learning participants were more likely to have employment in service-related fields than were volunteers. Service learning participation in college was shown to predict attitude toward both personal and community responsibility for improving the welfare of others. Because there are few studies of adult participants in service learning, much remains to be learned about how—and *if*—service learning can promote adult development.

There are a number of perspectives regarding the developmental changes that occur across the adult years. Theorists generally consider these domains to be significant to adult development:

- *Cognitive* (for example, knowledge acquisition and organization, information processing abilities, growth of intellectual skills and problem-solving abilities)
- *Moral, ethical, spiritual* (for example, ability to reason about moral and ethical issues, development of respect and tolerance, development of faith beliefs, consideration of meaning and purpose of life)
- *Social-emotional* (for example, autonomy, attachment relations, self-regulation, coping, generativity)
- *Physical* (for example, general health and well-being, involvement in health-sustaining activities such as exercise)
- *Cultural and civic* (for example, understanding social norms, role of laws, and customary practices in civil society; aesthetic appreciation; participation in civic activities such as voting)
- *Vocational* (for example, occupational exploration and development, skill building)

Growth within any domain may have effects on the other domains. For example, there is much overlap between cognitive and moral development (Kohlberg, 1976). There is emerging evidence that participation in service learning positively affects the cognitive and intellectual development of youths (Billig and Klute, 2003) and their sense of civic responsibility and engagement (Scales, Blyth, Berkas, and Kielsmeier, 2000). Service learning has been shown to contribute to improvements in self-concept and tolerance for others (Morgan and Streb, 2001), build leadership skills (Billig, 2002), and influence moral development (Conrad and Hedin, 1991) and a sense of ethics (Furco, 2002) among youth. Other research suggests the positive impact of service learning on students' development in areas such as personal efficacy, self-esteem, and confidence (Giles and Eyler, 1994), and it helps youths explore career options (Furco, 2002). It is not difficult to imagine, then, that service learning may have some similar benefits for adults—and perhaps other benefits as well.

New Directions for Adult and Continuing Education • DOI: 10.1002/ace

Service learning outcomes in three domains of adult development are considered in this chapter: cognitive growth, in terms of adults' ability to think in more complex ways and to consider a variety of perspectives; moral development, in terms of individuals developing an ethic of care (in other words, the ability to balance care of the self with the care of others); and psychosocial development, in terms of generativity (adults' ability to support and nurture the succeeding generation). Implications from three theoretical models are discussed: Robert Kegan's constructive-developmental theory of adult meaning making (1994), Carol Gilligan's care perspective on moral development (1982), and Erik Erikson's psychosocial perspective on generativity in middle adulthood (1982). Finally, suggestions for research on the impact of service learning in adult development are offered.

Dimensions of Service Learning

There are several dimensions of service learning courses and activities that are likely to have some bearing on adults' development. I briefly highlight four dimensions.

Duration. This dimension pertains to the length of time in which students participate in service learning, a "time-on-task" variable. Time-on-task is critical to learning (Brophy, 1988). The duration of participation may be brief (only a few total hours) or prolonged (dozens of hours of service accumulated over many weeks or months). Astin and Sax (1998) found that service duration, measured in terms of months, showed significant effects on thirty-four of thirty-five outcome measures among college freshmen, including students' academic development, life skill development, and civic responsibility. The effects of service duration on cognitive, moral, and psychosocial outcomes were not determined, however. Most service learning courses are of limited duration, so students' skills are not likely to be fully realized.

Scope. Scope is the breadth of opportunities to function in one's role as a service learning participant. Some service learning is relatively narrow (for example, picking up trash along a highway) while the scope of other activities may be quite broad (planning, organizing, and preparing and serving weekly meals at a homeless shelter). Although scope may be an important factor in individual motivation for service learning, it has not been investigated for adult students.

Intensity. Intensity pertains to students' affective responses to service learning. Service learning may be of relatively low emotional intensity (for example, working as a museum docent), or it may elicit strong affective responses (as in working with AIDS patients) on the part of learners. Students' affect can significantly contribute to their learning and cognition (Meyer and Turner, 2002); they remember more when the information to which they are exposed is emotionally charged (Heuer and Reisberg, 1992). The intensity dimension of service learning has not been investigated.

New Directions for Adult and Continuing Education • DOI: 10.1002/ace

Reflection. According to Eyler (2002), the amount and type of reflection in which students engage is an essential dimension of service learning. When students actively reflect on their service, they "discover the connections between actions and their effects" (Silcox, 1993, p. 2). Some courses require only a superficial level of reflection (daily logs of service learning activities), while others require students to engage in deep, systematic, and meaningful reflection (journaling) that helps to "identify, frame, and resolve ill-structured social problems" (Eyler, 2002, p. 523). Reflection has been extensively investigated in students' course learning (Eyler and Giles, 1999), but much less so for developmental outcomes.

Can Service Learning Contribute to Adults' Cognitive Growth?

As Eyler (2002) has noted, the capacity to "identify, frame, and resolve" complex social problems requires advanced cognitive development. Service learning courses that prompt reflection give students an opportunity to challenge their assumptions about social issues and analyze others' assumptions.

Constructive-Developmental Theory. Kegan (1994) described a constructive-developmental theory of adult cognitive growth that is useful to understanding adults' service learning experiences. Kegan's theory depicts six qualitatively distinct systems of thinking, or ways of knowing, in which individuals construct reality. The three most prevalent ways of knowing in adulthood are *instrumental, socializing,* and *self-authoring.* According to Drago-Severson (2004), instrumental knowers display cognitive egocentrism that orients them to their own interests, purposes, wants, and needs. They also view knowledge as something tangible and concrete, passed along by authority figures (in other words, teachers). They are motivated to acquire knowledge because it enables them to meet their needs and obtain instrumental outcomes (such as earning an A in a course). An instrumental knower's response to a service learning requirement is to ask, "What's in it for me?" It is unlikely that instrumental knowers can engage in the kinds of deep, sustained reflection that lead to real growth. The lack of reflective ability is related to the egocentric perspective of the instrumental knower. Instrumental knowers are likely to require direct guidance when reflecting on their service work, as well as instruction to consider the impact of their service on others.

Socializing knowers are oriented to others' expectations and opinions, and so gaining the acceptance of others and affiliating with them is important, according to Drago-Severson (2004). Socializing knowers view knowledge as what one should apply to fulfill social roles and meet the expectations of teachers and other authority figures. Not yet self-directed, the socializing knower's response to a service-learning requirement is to inquire of the teacher, "What do you think I should know (about service learning)?" They are motivated to participate in service learning because they believe that they will look good to others or because of the affiliative opportunities in such work.

Self-authoring knowers are oriented to their own internalized values and rely on these values to guide them. They are also concerned with their competence and performance—not how they appear to others. Because they see themselves as responsible for their own learning, the self-authoring knower's response to a service learning project is, "What do I need to learn about this activity, and how can I use this experience to keep learning and growing as a person?" They view service learning as an opportunity to improve their skills and knowledge or to enact the values they hold.

Developmental Transitions. Movement from one form of knowing to another occurs gradually, according to Kegan (1994), most likely taking years to achieve. These transitions require changes in individuals' perspective-taking abilities, as one must move from a self-centered to an other-oriented point of view and ultimately to a societal perspective. Research on service learning has not yet examined developmental transitions among adult learners, nor determined what events initiate these transitions. Few studies have observed service learning students for longer than a single semester to learn if their experiences eventually lead to more mature ways of knowing.

Can Service Learning Contribute to Adults' Moral Development?

There is evidence that service learning programs can have positive effects on students' moral reasoning skills (Boss, 1994; Conrad and Hedin, 1982). Studies show that service learning contributes to an increased sense of ethics—in other words, willingness to stand up for and do what is right (Furco, 2002) and greater social responsibility (Rosenberg, McKeon, and Dinero, 1999) on the part of students. Billig, Meyer, and Hofschire (2003) report that students involved in service learning are more likely to want to help others.

Concern for the well-being of others is an important dimension of moral development, according to Gilligan (1982), who has been a critic of Kohlberg's cognitive-structural theory of moral development (1976), which centers on application of principles of justice, concern for fairness, protection of personal rights, and meeting societal obligations. Viewing this "justice perspective" as limited, Gilligan and her colleagues interviewed girls and young women about personal decisions that contained a moral dimension (for example, having an abortion). Gilligan found that women demonstrate a different orientation to morality: the "care perspective." This ethic entails balancing responsibility to self and others with the need for self-protection, and it orients the individual toward establishing and nurturing relationships.

Pratt (2001) examined the relationship of service learning participation to moral development in a sample of male and female college students who

New Directions for Adult and Continuing Education • DOI: 10.1002/ace

did or did not participate in service learning. Both justice and care perspectives were assessed. No significant difference was observed between service learning and nonservice learning groups regarding moral reasoning. Men and women appeared to differ, however, in regard to moral orientation, although not moral reasoning. Service learning participation may have been too brief to affect change in moral reasoning.

Service learning presents many opportunities for adult participants to develop and maintain close relationships with other people, give care to those in need, and balance one's needs with a responsibility to care for others. It seems possible that engagement in service learning might, therefore, contribute to an "ethic of care" as a consequence of being in a helping, caregiver, or service provider role.

Can Service Learning Contribute to Adults' Psychosocial Maturity?

Psychosocial maturity is present when the individual has achieved autonomy and a sense of social responsibility (Greenberger, 1984). Autonomy is one's ability to function competently on one's own. Social responsibility is the ability to participate "in ensuring the well-being and survival of society [through] economically productive, socially integrative and self-protective work" (Greenberger, 1984, p. 4). A particularly relevant dimension of psychosocial maturity is development of generativity among adults. Autonomy is a precursor to generativity (Erikson, 1959), and social responsibility is an expression of it.

Generativity. Generativity concerns the ability to care for and provide for the next generation. According to McAdams, Hart, and Maruna (1998), generativity "consists of a constellation of inner desire, cultural demand, conscious concern, belief, commitment, action, and narration" that revolve around the psychosocial goal of being able to ensure the well-being, development, and survival of the species (p. 9). There are numerous ways in which adults can be generative. Young adults demonstrate the *desire* to be generative, according to Stewart and Vandewater (1998), but generativity can be accomplished only in middle and later adulthood.

Service learning activities for adult learners offer a potentially appealing framework for expressions of generativity. It may be possible for service learning to help adults achieve many of their generative goals. This hypothesis is as yet untested; no studies have examined the impact of service learning on generative desires, goals, or accomplishments.

Service Learning Dimensions and Adult Development

A number of questions about the relationship among the various dimensions, or qualities, of service learning courses and activities and adults' development within the cognitive, moral, and psychosocial domains can be generated, as shown in Table 1.1. In general, educators know that when

Table 1.1. Dimensions of Service Learning and Adult Cognitive, Moral, and Psychosocial Development

Domain	Duration	Scope	Intensity	Reflection
Cognitive Development Instrumental ------- Socializing ------- Self-Authoring	Does time-on-task contribute to helping adults advance from instrumental to socializing and self-authoring ways of knowing?	Does the scope of service-learning activities help adults advance from instrumental to socializing and self-authoring ways of knowing?	Does the affective intensity of the service-learning experience promote development from instrumental to socializing and self-authoring ways of knowing?	Does the depth of reflection required in service-learning courses help adults advance from instrumental to socializing and self-authoring ways of knowing?
Moral-Ethical Development Justice ------- Care	Does time-on-task contribute to advancing adults' moral development?	Does the scope of service-learning activities advance adults' moral reasoning skills?	Does the affective intensity of the service-learning experience advance adults' moral reasoning skills?	Does the depth of reflection required in service-learning courses advance adults' moral reasoning skills?
Psychosocial Development Generative Desires ------- Goals ------- Achievements	Does time-on-task contribute to helping adults' to establish generative goals and accomplish these goals?	Does the scope of service-learning activities promote development of adults' generative goals?	Does the affective intensity of the service-learning experience promote development of adults' generative goals?	Does the depth of reflection required in service-learning courses help adults to develop generative goals and accomplish these goals?

students spend more time on task—all things being equal—they learn more. But does more time spent in a given learning activity serve to promote adult development? The answer to this question is not readily apparent from the extant service learning research. Similarly, researchers have not yet addressed the issues of how the scope of service learning activities and the affective intensity of these experiences may help to promote adults' cognitive, moral, and psychosocial developments. The requirement for students to reflect on their service learning experience has been extensively studied, however (Eyler, 2002). Yet, as Eyler notes, "We know reflection is a good thing—but we don't know how to structure reflection and integrate it with service to maximize learning—or what that learning might look like" (n.p.). Nor do we know specifically how reflection contributes to cognitive, moral, or psychosocial development.

Conclusions

I have speculated about the possible impact of service learning within three domains of adult development: cognitive, moral-ethical, and psychosocial. Several dimensions of service learning—its duration, scope, and intensity, and the extent to which students' personal reflection about their experiences is required—may play important roles in adult development. Advocates of service learning have established a body of research that is suggestive of the impact exerted by service learning on K–16 students' academic achievement, moral development, interpersonal skills and socialization, and citizenship participation. Adult learners' academic goals, their reasons for participating in adult education, and the outcomes of their academic pursuits are often quite different from those of younger students, however (Knowles, 1984). Yet there is little reason to anticipate that adult learners would not benefit, in similar ways, from participating in service learning activities. Unfortunately, there is scant research on how nontraditional and older adult students fare as a result of participating in service learning as a part of their coursework.

Studies of service learning should investigate how these experiences foster cognitive growth among adult participants. In particular, what are the specific elements of these experiences that lead to increased critical thinking, problem solving, and reflection? Research is needed that focuses on how service learning can promote individual development from instrumental to self-authoring ways of knowing among participants. The available evidence is mixed at best regarding the effects of service learning on students' moral reasoning. Few studies have used experimental designs where students have been randomly assigned to service learning or nonservice learning conditions. Adult educators should also seek to determine if service learning experiences foster an ethic of care among participants. Studies can also investigate if and how service learning contributes to

New Directions for Adult and Continuing Education • DOI: 10.1002/ace

younger, middle-aged, and older adult students' generativity desires, goals, and accomplishments. Does service learning satisfy generative desires? Do adult participants feel more generative as a result of their involvement in service learning? Aside from age, attention should also be paid to other characteristics of adult learners.

Attention should be devoted to the dimensions of service learning courses that may affect learners' experiences—duration, scope, intensity, and reflection. Service learning courses are constrained by academic institutions' quarter and semester schedules. Yet even within a brief time period, it is possible to study developmental processes. Granott (1998), for example, advocates study of microdevelopmental processes—that is, development that takes place over a short time span (hours or days). This approach requires precise, frequent measurement of the relevant developmental processes. Thus the brief duration of service learning courses should not be an impediment to studying developmental changes.

Reflection has been advocated as the primary tool for learners to intellectually benefit from service learning. It helps adults critically analyze the assumptions and attitudes that underlie their knowledge. But less well understood are the specific mechanisms by which cognitive reflection about service learning has an impact on adults' cognitive skills—to say nothing of moral reasoning, or generative goals and actions. Studies must determine what kinds of reflective activities work well to affect adult learners' cognitive change.

Because there are few studies involving nontraditional and older adult learners in service learning, adult educators should proceed cautiously in developing service learning requirements for adult students and avoid making unsubstantiated claims as to the benefits of service learning for adults.

References

Astin, A. W., and Sax, L. J. "How Undergraduates Are Affected by Service Participation." *Journal of College Student Development,* 1998, *39*(3), 251–263.

Billig, S. H. *Philadelphia Freedom Schools Junior Leader Evaluation.* Denver, Colo.: RMC Research, 2002.

Billig, S. H., and Klute, M. M. "The Impact of Service-Learning on MEAP: A Large-Scale Study of Michigan Learn and Serve Grantees." Presentation at National Service-Learning Conference, Minneapolis, Minn., April 2003.

Billig, S. H., Meyer, S., and Hofschire, L. "Evaluation of Center for Research on Education, Diversity, and Excellence Demonstration Site, the Hawaiian Studies Program at Waianae High School." Denver, Colo.: RMC Research, 2003.

Boss, J. A. "The Effect of Community Service on the Moral Development of College Ethics Students." *Journal of Moral Education,* 1994, *23*(2), 183–198.

Brophy, J. E. "Research Linking Teacher Behavior to Student Achievement: Potential Implications for Instruction of Chapter 1 Students." *Educational Psychologist,* 1988, *23,* 235–286.

Conrad, D., and Hedin, D. "The Impact of Experiential Education on Adolescent Development." *Child and Youth Services*, 1982, 4(3/4), 57–76.

Conrad, D., and Hedin, D. "School-Based Community Service: What We Know from Research and Theory." *Phi Delta Kappan*, 1991, June, 743–749.

Conrad, D., and Hedin, D. "School-Based Community Service: What We Know from Research and Theory." Retrieved online Aug. 8, 2005, at http://www.lionsquest.org/content/Resources/ServiceLearningArticles/slarticle17.htm.

Drago-Severson, E. *Becoming Adult Learners: Principles and Practices for Effective Development.* New York: Teachers College Press, 2004.

Erikson, E. H. *Identity and the Life Cycle.* New York: Norton, 1959.

Erikson, E. H. *The Life Cycle Completed.* New York: Norton, 1982.

Eyler, J. "Reflection: Linking Service and Learning-Linking Students and Communities." *Journal of Social Issues*, 2002, 58(3), 517–534.

Eyler, J. S. "What Do We Most Need to Know About the Impact of Service-Learning on Student Learning?" *Michigan Journal of Community & Service-Learning*, 2000. Retrieved online Oct. 6, 2005, at http://www.umich.edu/~mjcsl/volumes/2000sample.html.

Eyler, J. S., and Giles Jr., D. E. *Where's the Learning in Service-Learning?* San Francisco: Jossey-Bass, 1999.

Fenzel, M. L., Peyrot, M., Speck, S., and Gugerty, C. "Distinguishing Attitudinal and Behavioral Differences Among College Alumni Who Have Participated in Service-Learning and Volunteer Service." Paper presented at annual meeting of American Educational Research Association, Chicago, April 2003.

Furco, A. "Is Service-Learning Really Better Than Community Service? A Study of High School Service." In A. Furco and S. H. Billig (eds.), *Advances in Service-Learning Research,* Vol. 1. *Service-Learning: The Essence of the Pedagogy.* Greenwich, Conn.: Information Age, 2002.

Giles Jr., D. E., and Eyler, J. "The Impact of a College Community Service Laboratory on Students' Personal, Social, and Cognitive Outcomes." *Journal of Adolescence*, 1994, 17(4), 327–339.

Gilligan, C. *In a Different Voice.* Cambridge, Mass.: Harvard University Press, 1982.

Granott, N. "We Learn, Therefore We Develop: Learning Versus Development—or Developing Learning?" In M C. Smith and T. Pourchot (eds.), *Adult Learning and Development: Perspectives from Educational Psychology.* Mahwah, N.J.: Erlbaum, 1998.

Greenberger, E. "Defining Psychosocial Maturity in Adolescence." In P. J. Karoly and J. J. Steffens (eds.), *Adolescent Behavior Disorders: Foundations and Contemporary Concerns. Advances in Child Behavioral Analysis and Therapy,* Vol. 3. Lexington, Mass.: Lexington Books, 1984.

Heuer, F., and Reisberg, D. "Emotion, Arousal, and Memory for Detail." In S. Christianson (ed.), *Handbook of Emotion and Memory.* Hillsdale, N.J.: Erlbaum, 1992.

Kegan, R. G. *In over Our Heads: The Mental Demands of Modern Life.* Cambridge, Mass.: Harvard University Press, 1994.

Kohlberg, L. "Moral Stages and Moralization: The Cognitive-Developmental Approach." In T. Lickona (ed.), *Moral Development and Behavior.* Austin, Tex.: Holt, Rinehart, & Winston, 1976.

Knowles, M. *The Adult Learner: A Neglected Species.* Malabar, Fla.: Gulf, 1984.

McAdams, D. P., Hart, H. M., and Maruna, S. "The Anatomy of Generativity." In D. P. McAdams and E. de St. Aubin (eds.), *Generativity and Adult Development: How and Why We Care for the Next Generation.* Washington, D.C.: American Psychological Association, 1998.

Meyer, D. K., and Turner, J. C. "Discovering Emotion in Classroom Motivation Research." *Educational Psychologist*, 2002, 37, 107–114.

Morgan, W., and Streb, M. "Building Citizenship: How Student Voice in Service-Learning Develops Civic Values." *Social Science Quarterly*, 2001, 82(1), 155–169.

Pratt, S. B. "Moral Development in College Students Engaged in Community Service Learning: A Justice-Care Perspective." Unpublished doctoral dissertation, Boston College, 2001.

Rosenberg, S. L., McKeon, L. M., and Dinero, T. E. "Positive Peer Solutions: One Answer for the Rejected Student." Phi Delta Kappan, 1999, 81(2), 114–118. Retrieved online Sept. 13, 2005, at http://www.pklintl.org/kappan/kros9910.htm.

Scales, P. C., Blyth, D. A., Berkas, T. H., and Kielsmeier, J. C. "The Effects of Service-Learning on Middle School Students' Social Responsibility and Academic Success." Journal of Early Adolescence, 2000, 20(3), 332–358.

Silcox, H. C. A How-to Guide to Reflection: Adding Cognitive Learning to Community Service Programs. Philadelphia: Brighton Press, 1993.

Stewart, A. J., and Vandewater, E. "The Course of Generativity." In D. P. McAdams and E. de St. Aubin (eds.), Generativity and Adult Development: How and Why We Care for the Next Generation. Washington, D.C.: American Psychological Association, 1998.

Vogelgesang, L., and Astin, A. "Comparing the Effects of Community Service and Service-Learning." Michigan Journal of Community Service-Learning, Fall 2000, 7, 25–34.

M. CECIL SMITH is a professor of educational psychology at Northern Illinois University. His research interests pertain to adults' literacy practices and skills. He is currently editing the Handbook of Research on Adulthood: Adult Development and Learning.

New Directions for Adult and Continuing Education • DOI: 10.1002/ace

2

Beyond the classroom, adults are benefiting from learning through community involvement as a component of career or retirement activities.

Community Based Learning with Adults: Bridging Efforts in Multiple Sectors

Barbara Holland, Gail Robinson

In this chapter, we explore the diverse ways in which community based learning strategies are used to enhance further development of adults, raising their levels of educational attainment and increasing their involvement in public and civic activities. There are two social and demographic dynamics at the heart of this topic: the aging profile of the American population; and the need, among employers, educators, and nonprofits, to energize and motivate more people to be active in community and civic matters that are essential to community improvement and problem solving (Eisner and Cohen, 2006). Many types of organizations offer programs that give adults the opportunity to become more active in a community, and some link learning with action to enhance development of adults' values, knowledge, and skills.

In postsecondary education, the changing age demographic means that students attending college or university are increasingly older, with most working many hours, living off campus, dealing with family responsibilities, and commuting among home, work, and school. In addition, the increasing cost of tuition and other economic pressures encourage students to postpone enrolling after high school, and they may "stop out" of college occasionally to work more and save money. Students meeting these characteristics have more than a 55 percent probability of being among those who depart early and without credentials (Jacobs and Hundley, 2005). This chapter explores how community based learning strategies address the needs of these students and improve their success rate.

NEW DIRECTIONS FOR ADULT AND CONTINUING EDUCATION, no. 118, Summer 2008 © 2008 Wiley Periodicals, Inc.
Published online in Wiley InterScience (www.interscience.wiley.com) • DOI: 10.1002/ace.292

In the workplace, business and corporate success is inspiring greater attention to corporate citizenship. There has clearly been a recent increase in business support for employee involvement in the community through employee volunteer programs and other activities meant to demonstrate corporate social responsibility. These initiatives also have the potential to contribute to employee professional development and retention. We offer examples and ideas for future developments in this chapter.

On a national scale, there is much discussion about the social and economic implications of the aging baby boomer group. Will they all retire rapidly, creating a shortage of skills and workers? Will they retire slowly and remain in the workforce longer? Whichever scenario develops, research shows that boomers do not want a retirement that resembles that of their parents; they want to be active and busy. We describe several programs designed to involve older adults in community action projects and discuss their potential impact.

First, it is important for the reader to understand the terms used in the chapter. *Service learning,* sometimes called *community based learning,* combines service activities with academic learning objectives with the intent that the activity will benefit both the recipient and the provider. The connection between the service tasks and learning is facilitated by structured reflections that explore key issues of knowledge, skills, and values, as well as specific dimensions especially relevant to the particular activity (National Service-Learning Clearinghouse, 2007).

Service learning has expanded rapidly over the last twenty years. The number of institutions belonging to Campus Compact, the number receiving support from the Learn and Serve America federal grant program, and the statistics given here regarding community colleges suggest it is safe to estimate that more than a third of all U.S. postsecondary institutions are using service learning. A larger and broader movement that led many colleges and universities to develop an agenda of community engagement fuels the growth of this learning strategy.

The idea of community engagement in higher education is rooted in awareness that postsecondary institutions have moral and civic responsibilities, as well as intellectual reasons, for ensuring that their teaching and research activities are contributing in some direct way to the important questions of the economy, society, culture, health, safety, and the environment. In 2006, the Carnegie Foundation for the Advancement of Teaching launched an elective institutional classification model that allows institutions to be categorized according to their level of commitment to engagement. This attention to classification of engaged institutions is evidence of the engagement's extensive institutionalization across the higher education sector (Carnegie, 2006). In the context of engagement, service learning is a mode of engaged teaching and an important element of any academic institution's engagement agenda.

New Directions for Adult and Continuing Education • DOI: 10.1002/ace

Service learning is most often and most effectively integrated into credit-bearing courses and strongly linked to specific learning objectives. In other words, the decision to use a service learning model would be driven by the instructor's belief that certain academic, social, civic, personal, or professional learning goals cannot be met unless the students engage in a community based project.

As distinguished from traditional models of out-of-classroom learning (internships, practica, clinical training, workplace learning), service learning has at its core the expectation that the activity be meaningful and valuable to both the student doing the service and the community members partnering on the service projects. Even though all traditional forms of out-of-classroom learning are valuable and important, this model creates a learning environment where students are learning from their interactions with community partners or residents because the community members have unique knowledge to teach the students. Rather than merely send students out to do "good works" or service projects for their own sake, or to take an internship that is focused primarily on their own professional development, this model is based on partner strategies that require the students and community to interact so as to promote a knowledge exchange relationship.

In the context of educational institutions, service learning is the most commonly used term; however, some postsecondary institutions may have academic cultural values that associate the word *service* with activities that are not intellectually rigorous. In those settings, the term *community based learning* is often used but means the same thing and operates with the same principles.

Both community based and service learning can be distinguished by these characteristics: (1) clear learning objectives that connect classroom learning to community based learning, (2) service activities that address a community-identified need, (3) community partners who act as co-educators and contribute to student learning, (4) an activity that ensures benefits to both the student and the community with an exchange of knowledge that strengthens both parties, (5) connections to the learning goals established through rigorous and intellectually challenging reflection activities, and (6) consequential assessment strategies capturing student learning outcomes and informing partnership improvement.

Outside of educational organizations, the phrase community based learning is increasingly used to describe activities organized through the workplace, through social organizations, or diverse types of adult development, personal improvement, and professional development venues. There is little documentation of this relatively new phenomenon, but we explore some of the evidence and examples available and offer some conjecture as to where community based learning strategies could go in terms of enriching the lives of adults, promoting lifelong learning, and increasing the adult volunteer rate across society, all to the betterment of community quality of life.

Community Based Learning in Postsecondary Education

Not long after the first U.S. community college was founded in 1901, and largely on the basis of John Dewey's work in the early part of the twentieth century, colleges and universities began incorporating more experiential learning into academic course work: learning by doing. The remarkable growth in establishing new community colleges in the 1960s and 1970s paralleled an increase in community based learning. But the majority of service learning programs, more than 80 percent among community colleges for example, began in 1990 or later (Robinson and Barnett, 1996).

As one indicator of this growth, Campus Compact, a nationwide institutional membership organization supporting civic engagement and service learning, grew from a few institutional members in 1986 to more than 1,000 at the time of its twentieth anniversary in 2006. During 2006, more than a third of the students attending Compact member institutions were engaged in service learning programs, providing almost 400 million hours in service to communities (Campus Compact, 2006).

Much more important than hours of service, research to date also links service learning with improved student retention; academic learning (acquisition and retention of content, grade point average); persistence to degree completion; and increases in prosocial behaviors, self-esteem, motivation, critical thinking and communications skills, and interpersonal relationships, including multicultural and global understanding (Eyler, Giles, Stenson, and Gray, 2001). The benefits of service learning for students can be clustered around personal, social, civic, academic, and career learning outcomes.

Will Busy Students Have Time to Be Engaged? To some academic leaders, it is surprising that community based learning has grown so quickly given the increasingly overloaded and complex lives contemporary students lead, as we have just described. The traditional student (white, well-prepared, living on campus, carrying a full course load, and finishing in four years) is a vanishing breed and should now be considered nontraditional. The old notion of the nontraditional student is now the traditional, as more than half of students currently enrolled attend part-time and plan intentionally to take six years or more to complete a baccalaureate degree.

As a result, faculty and administrators are often quick to assume that these working, commuting students are too busy to fit community based learning into their crowded schedules. Students may also say they are too busy to participate in service learning, thanks to their work and family responsibilities. However, these objections have been disproved by research on student experience. In surveys of students in the California State University System, one of the largest in the nation, several questions were asked about participation in service learning. Students who worked reported a higher level of participation in service learning courses (S. Eckardt, personal communication, Nov. 4, 2005). A similar survey of students at Occidental

College (California), a small private college, produced similar results (M. Avila, personal communication, Nov. 28, 2005).

It is human nature that if we are really busy, the suggestion of a new activity seems unattractive to us at first. However, if the idea is presented appropriately to show the benefits and return on time invested for our participation in a new activity, we may be more interested. Over the last twenty years, a great deal has been learned about implementing service learning in differing institutional settings, including those serving students with characteristics that put them at risk of dropping out or otherwise failing to complete their studies. Practice demonstrates that if the concept of community based learning is presented by an instructor as an integral part of course expectations, students will accept it as an assignment that must be completed. Anecdotal evidence suggests that once students try community based learning, they resonate with it powerfully and often ask for more such experiences. Surveys of students reveal that they appreciate the practicality and relevance of community based learning and see it as transformative (Gelmon, Holland, and Shinnamon, 1998). Through direct experience of well-designed activities, students learn that community based learning need not be a burden; indeed, it offers great academic and personal rewards (Graham and Donaldson, 1999). This aligns with the greater interest of the contemporary student in active learning pedagogies, as Generation X and millennial students make it clear they want to see more direct connection between learning and experience (Yankelovich, 2005).

Community Colleges. The increased use of service learning or community based learning extends across all types of postsecondary institutions. Community colleges have launched many community based learning initiatives for adults, as they meet their mission of community service while educating 46 percent of all undergraduates in the United States. With an average student age of twenty-nine, most community college students work full-time or part-time and have caretaking responsibilities for younger and older family members.

These students lead the way in looking for more engaged types of teaching and learning, whether through internships, clinical or practicum experiences, or service learning. According to four national surveys conducted by the American Association of Community Colleges (AACC) between 1995 and 2003, nearly 60 percent of all community colleges offer service learning as part of academic course work.

Studies of community college students demonstrate their positive response to community based learning. In 1999 and 2000, AACC surveyed more than one thousand students at fourteen institutions participating in its Learn and Serve America grant program (Robinson and Henderson, 2000). Students reported that their service learning experiences affected the following "a lot" or "some": improved grade point average (58 percent), desire to stay in college and complete degree (58 percent), development of occupational skills (79 percent), ability to work and learn independently

New Directions for Adult and Continuing Education • DOI: 10.1002/ace

(83 percent), positive attitude toward community involvement and citizenship (90 percent), and connection of course subject matter with everyday life (90 percent).

In another AACC study from 2004 through 2006, 368 service learning students at ten colleges reported a higher level of civic engagement than nonservice learners (Prentice and Robinson, 2007). After taking courses that offered service learning, 71 percent of those students reported that service learning increased their knowledge of community needs and how people can address them. In addition, 59 percent reported an increased commitment to continue serving in their communities.

Service learning students also reported on the academic impact of service learning. Sixty-five percent said that the service aspect of their courses helped them see how the subject matter they learned can be used in everyday life. Ninety-three percent believed that the idea of combining course work with service to the community should be practiced in more college courses.

Three themes supporting the 2004–2006 survey data emerged from postsurvey focus groups at the participating institutions. Service learning participation increased students' knowledge of community needs as well as where to go for solutions. It also increased students' commitment to continue being involved in the community after they finished college. Finally, participation in service learning helped students have a better understanding of their role as community members.

Reflection, as was described earlier, is a key to connecting service to learning in community based learning models. Through reflection, adult learners see the value in learning in community based settings. One student who participated in the 2006 AACC civic engagement focus groups said: "Service learning made me feel that the stuff I was learning in class meant more. It gave it meaning and everything. Maybe in the classes that I don't necessarily feel interested in or have a hard time in, I may do service learning for those classes, so I can put more meaning into what I'm trying to learn" (Prentice and Robinson, 2006). Another said: "Participating in the service learning program has helped me to define my role in the community. I now know that I can do something other than teach. I can make senior citizens laugh. I can get them to talk. So it's added another dimension to who I am."

Because community colleges serve almost half of all postsecondary students in the United States, this evidence that it is improving retention, awareness of community issues, and their motivation to be actively involved in communities is good news.

Universities. Among comprehensive and research universities, primarily regionally oriented public and private universities that mainly served adult students from their immediate area adopted community based learning strategies (Holland, 2005). This dominance of participation by local students influences the academic values and cultures of these universities

New Directions for Adult and Continuing Education • DOI: 10.1002/ace

intensely because students bring the community to the classroom with them. The more that instructional design integrates and uses community experience, the more students will learn and retain.

Similar to community colleges, students at many of America's universities also are adult learners who lead time-poor lives with competing demands for work, family, commuting, and academic study. In fact, most traditional-aged students (eighteen to twenty-two) have taken on the characteristics of what we think of as adult learners as they are compelled to cope with similarly complex, multidimensional, and demanding life strategies (Tinto, 1999). However, much more than community colleges, four-year colleges and universities are challenged by historical expectations and stereotypes about university student behavior, especially the notion that students should put their studies paramount in organizing their lives. Adopting effective strategies such as service learning or community based learning requires significant changes in organizational structures and academic culture to achieve support and buy-in from faculty.

Fortunately, there has been extensive study of strategies and models for encouraging universities to adopt community based learning for their students. Evidence of its benefits was presented earlier in this chapter. For adult learners in particular, engagement enhances the relevance of instruction and imparts benefits to academic, social, and civic learning as well as professional development in some cases (Richter-Hauk and Arias, Chapter Three of this volume; Graham and Donaldson, 1999; Eyler and Giles, 1999). Heard (2005) suggested five strategies for implementing community based learning for adult learners: (1) give adult students purposeful (not abstract) assignments and activities, (2) present a variety of engaging learning models and experiences, (3) help adult students discover the link between academic learning and their future success, (4) include adult students in institutional governance and recognize their skills, and (5) offer training for faculty to increase their knowledge of adult learners (Heard, 2005).

Success in involving adult learners in community based learning has even extended to a few examples of their involvement in international service learning. At the University of Louisville, adult learners find international study compatible with their learning goals and objectives and appreciate the opportunity to experience other cultures (often for the first time) and gain confidence from applying their newly acquired knowledge to the benefit of others (Gifford, Strenecky, and Cunningham, 2005).

From evidence of its effectiveness in promoting better learning and retention outcomes, community based learning now thrives at every type and level of academic institution: K–12 schools, community colleges, liberal arts colleges, comprehensive four-year institutions, and research universities. This growth is now expanding community based learning into graduate study and is already shaping the future of the next generation of faculty, many of whom will come from today's adult learners.

New Directions for Adult and Continuing Education • DOI: 10.1002/ace

Adults Learning "in" the Community: An Engaged Leadership Institute Model

Central New Mexico Community College created a program that emphasized civic engagement while preparing participants to work with diverse groups of people and environments in learning how to address community issues. Based on the LeadershipPlenty program of the Pew Partnership for Civic Change, Central New Mexico's Civic Engagement Leadership Institute (CELI) began in 2002. Participants were students, faculty, staff, and community members. They met weekly over a three-month period, working on such topics as finding leaders within themselves, identifying community assets, managing conflict, and building partnerships.

By the end of its second year, CELI had a 97 percent retention rate for its participants. End-of-year data indicated that 75 percent of participants remained involved in service work, 95 percent strongly agreed the institute improved their interpersonal skills development, 90 percent had a better understanding of dimensions of diversity, 98 percent strongly agreed the institute improved their ability to work in teams, and 96 percent agreed the institute gave them the skills necessary to address community issues. In the third year of CELI, the program shifted to focus on Spanish-speaking members of the Albuquerque area, who requested this program be offered in Spanish. Many of the participants were parents who wanted to be more involved in their children's schools. This unique adult learning opportunity increased participants' confidence in their skills as involved parents and community members.

Boasting a 100 percent retention rate for participants, end-of-year data showed that 100 percent remained involved in service work, 98 percent strongly agreed CELI improved their interpersonal skills development and had a better understanding of diversity dimensions, and 100 percent agreed the institute improved their ability to work in teams and gave them the skills necessary to address community issues. The success of CELI depended on administrative support for leadership and civic engagement, commitment of institute facilitators for campus-community partnerships, and knowledge of and comfort with experiential exercises.

Adult Learning in the Workplace

As community based learning opportunities grow in higher education, they are being offered in the corporate world as well. A growing number of businesses and corporations sponsor employee volunteer programs (EVP). An EVP is "a planned, managed effort that seeks to motivate and enable employees to volunteer effectively under the sponsorship and leadership of the employer" (Points of Light Foundations, 2004). They range from Home Depot supplying materials for staff to build new homes for victims of

New Directions for Adult and Continuing Education • DOI: 10.1002/ace

Hurricane Katrina to Microsoft employees receiving training on how to serve on local nonprofit boards.

According to the Points of Light Foundation (POLF), more than twenty-five hundred U.S. corporations and businesses offer skills-based and other volunteer opportunities to their workers. In 2005, POLF began an award program for Excellence in Workplace Volunteer Programs. Some give their employees a set number of hours as "release time" to volunteer on their own. Others organize group volunteer events around national days of service such as Global Volunteer Day and the Martin Luther King, Jr., Day of Service. Still others take up a specific issue or topic, such as tutoring programs to improve reading in schools. Clearly, at a minimum EVPs furnish human and capital resources to nonprofit organizations that may also be helping employees and their families, attract better employees and increase retention, build employee morale and loyalty, and address employee work/life issues (POLF, 2004).

A less explored but intriguing question is, Could EVPs also offer professional development opportunities for employees across the workforce spectrum? If community based learning improves learning outcomes for postsecondary education students, would it not also contribute to further development of employees, especially if the design of EVPs aligned with the proven practices of community based learning strategies? Interest on the part of employees should certainly be sufficient; the growing prevalence of skill-based volunteering shows that more people want to use their existing skills, or improve on what they already know, in service to others (Wilson and Simson, 2006).

Without new research, we cannot yet answer these questions about the link between quality EVPs that offer employees skill-based volunteering opportunities and employee professional development. In reviewing the examples they have collected, POLF suggested there are five factors that may be important to "ensuring that an employee skill-based volunteer program is successful at developing workplace skills": full compliance with adult learner theory, a team approach, sound support structures, financial resources, and process and outcome evaluation (POLF, 2007).

A look at the POLF award nominees revealed that the managers of EVPs prepare their employees for their service experience by acquainting them with the service sites and their programs and familiarizing them with the types of clients or families with whom they may interact. This is quite similar to the way college faculty members prepare their students for community based learning. However, few of these programs incorporate formal or informal reflection following group service activities. Note that, unlike at educational institutions, many EVP managers have not discovered reflection is the key to gaining the learning and professional development outcomes that community based activity can produce. Without intentional reflection, gains may not appear in the participating employees. Two examples of EVP reflection or near-reflection are KPMG LLP, an international accounting and consulting firm that places more extensive emphasis on pre-service preparation than postservice reflection; and Walt Disney, where a community partner leads reflection activities for employees who work with Kids Care Clubs on Family Volunteer Days.

To advance adult learning in EVPs, preparation and reflection can help managers glean suggestions for program improvement, allow employees to consider the short-term impact of their volunteer service, and plan more long-term strategies for serving and learning. Preparation focuses participant attention on the purpose of the activity, the knowledge and skills required to do it well, and the developmental opportunities or learning goals it presents. Reflection offers adult volunteers the opportunity for groups and individual learners to assess the impact of their experience and how it has contributed to their personal and professional abilities and motivations.

Sadly, there are few cases where colleges and universities offer organized EVPs to their own faculty, staff, and administrators. Northern Kentucky University launched a modest EVP program in 2000 that created a one-day special community service day with all participants working on a major project developed with community (such as painting all the classrooms in a community school), and also allows some release time for other volunteer activities as individuals. An advantage of this model is that it gives academic and professional staff a positive way to work together and enjoy the results of their work.

Paired with community service or service learning programs, EVPs can have a tremendous impact on academic or corporate organizations in the short run and long run. Benefits could include conducting teamwork activities, offering leadership development opportunities, enhancing communication skills, supplying employee and management training and skill building, strengthening relationships with local constituents, assisting in alleviating community problems and issues, attracting new students or employees from the community, developing action-oriented relationships with community leaders, and creating new partnerships with the philanthropic sector.

EVPs can afford adult learners in all kinds of settings a wealth of options for learning while giving, and we predict they will continue to grow as large organizations, public and private, see the benefit of demonstrating their citizenship role in their local community and the employee benefits gained through such work.

Baby Boomers and Volunteering

By 2030, one in five Americans will be sixty-five years old. The Corporation for National and Community Service, especially its Senior Corps program, is working to create strategies that will prepare and attract baby boomers into the volunteer workforce, even before their full retirement has begun. As the nonprofit and profit sectors have begun to plan for the impact of the

New Directions for Adult and Continuing Education • DOI: 10.1002/ace

exit of baby boomers from the workforce, research is being conducted on their attitudes and probable behaviors as volunteers.

Interview research conducted by the Center on Aging at the University of Maryland produced findings that help inform current community based learning strategies in education, the workplace, and community settings where volunteers are needed. First and foremost, they found that baby boomers don't want to become old; they actively resist being referred to as older, senior, or retired. They expect their service in community to be meaningful, challenging, and drawing on their skills, almost like professional consulting. Efforts to recruit volunteers will have to indicate the organization is offering opportunities that demand high skills. The researchers also found that many volunteer networks are already going to corporations and businesses to encourage EVPs and suggest part-time or part-retirement models that will help encourage baby boomers to consider work and service in community settings as a "second career" activity and a strategy for lifelong learning (Wilson and Simson, 2006). Such strategies offer a hopeful vision for more seamless connections between workplace employment and community service at any age, if EVP programs continue to emerge.

An AARP survey in 2000 found that, following retirement, adults do want to continue learning new things while also putting their extant knowledge and experience to work. As an example of programs that are combining recreation, learning, and productivity, Lewis (2002) wrote about transitions in the nature of Elderhostel programs, which increasingly offer hybrid programs with different choices of intensive trips that combine service and learning.

In response to baby boomer demand for lifelong learning in modes that suit their interests, the University of the Third Age (U3A), popular in the United Kingdom, is beginning to spread to the United States and elsewhere internationally. The model offers online and in-person learning opportunities for educational, creative, and leisure purposes; there is no assessment built in. In the United States, some U3A programs are collaborative with universities and colleges; others are community-organized hubs of learners who teach and learn from each other and are self-directed. The aims of U3A are to (1) encourage and enable older people no longer in full-time paid employment to help each other share their knowledge, skills, interests, and experience; (2) demonstrate the benefits and enjoyment to be gained and the new horizons to be discovered in learning throughout life; (3) celebrate the capabilities and potential of older people and their value to society; (4) make U3As accessible to all older people; and (5) encourage establishment of U3As in every part of the country where conditions are suitable and support and collaborate with them (see University of the Third Age at www.u3a.org.uk).

Unfortunately, the idea of community based learning or using knowledge to improve community conditions does not appear explicitly in the aims or purposes of U3A, but anecdotes in the United States suggest that

New Directions for Adult and Continuing Education • DOI: 10.1002/ace

some models do link learning and service. One analysis of the program suggests that participants' being self-organizing into teams, developing collaborative projects, and working across diverse economic and educational populations is a strategy for enhancing community leadership skills and will ultimately contribute to further community development (Hentschel and Eisen, 2002). We mention this growing initiative here to draw attention to it and to suggest, as with employee volunteer programs, it has important and untapped potential to increase social and civic engagement across the nation, especially among the baby boomers.

Putting It All Together Across the Generations

A specific approach to engaging baby boomers in community based learning activities is the Seniors and Youth Engaged in Service program (SaYES), co-sponsored by Learn and Serve America and Senior Corps, both programs of the Corporation for National and Community Service. SaYES furnishes training and technical assistance to schools and community based organizations to help them recruit and prepare individuals fifty-five and older who will serve as volunteers in schools and communities to assist in leading quality service-learning and youth service activities (NSLC, 2006).

The need for the program is great, as more and more schools are taking up service learning; the labor-intensive nature of organizing and managing community based learning activities for many children and youth can be daunting. Older adults have much to contribute by helping schools and community organizations access the human capacity and expertise they need to make these programs viable and sustainable. In the ideal, SaYES program models lead to seniors, baby boomers, and kids working side-by-side on community based projects that address critical issues. Feedback to date is that the program resonates with the interests of baby boomers as adult volunteers. The only complaint so far is the resistance to being called "seniors"!

Conclusion

Although service learning and community based learning are not the only answer, evidence suggests that they are an essential part of solving many challenges: responding effectively to adult learner needs and preferences, raising adult learner ambitions to further study and success, making education more inviting and inclusive for diverse adult learners, and making postsecondary and workplace learning more efficient and compelling by giving learning activities real purpose. Perhaps most important, community based learning is an effective tool for engaging learners of all ages in exploration of their values and the opportunities to be constructive and active participants in community affairs and public issues. A core underlying purpose of community based learning is that it has demonstrated its capacity

New Directions for Adult and Continuing Education • DOI: 10.1002/ace

to reenergize the uniquely American tradition of community service, volunteerism, and grassroots community action for learners across generations.

References

Campus Compact. "Campus Compact Annual Membership Survey, 2006." Providence, R.I.: Campus Compact, 2006.

Carnegie Foundation. "Community Engagement Elective Classifications," 2006 (http://www.carnegiefoundation.org/classifications/index.asp?key=1213).

Eisner, D., and Cohen, A. "Service and Civic-Engagement as a Common Expectation in Higher Education." In B. Holland and J. Meeropol (eds.), *A More Perfect Vision: The Future of Campus Engagement.* Providence, R.I.: Campus Compact, 2006 (http://www.compact.org/20th/papers).

Eyler, J. S., and Giles, D. E. *Where's the Learning in Service-Learning?* San Francisco: Jossey-Bass, 1999.

Eyler, J. S., Giles, D. E., Stenson, C. M., and Gray, C. J. *At a Glance: What We Know About the Effects of Service-Learning on College Students, Faculty, Institutions and Communities, 1993–2000* (3rd ed.). Washington D.C.: Learn and Serve America, Corporation for National and Community Service, 2001.

Gelmon, S. B., Holland, B. A., and Shinnamon, A. F. *Health Professions Schools in Service to the Nation: 1996–98 Final Evaluation Report.* San Francisco: Community-Campus Partnerships for Health, 1998 (http.//depts.washington.edu/ccph/guide.html#Publications).

Gifford, D. B., Strenecky, J., and Cunningham, H. R. (2005). "International Service Learning Successfully Engaging Adult Students." *Metropolitan Universities,* 2005, *16*(2), 53–62.

Graham, S. W., and Donaldson, D. J. "Effect of Involvement for Traditional Undergraduates." Paper presented at Forum for Institutional Research, Chicago, 1999.

Heard, J.D.T. "Engaging Adult Students." *Metropolitan Universities,* 2005, *16*(2), 45–52.

Hentschel, D., and Eisen, M. "Developing Older Adults as Community Leaders." *Adult Learning,* 2002, *13*(4), 12–14.

Holland, B. A. "Institutional Differences in Pursuing the Public Good." In A. J. Kezar, T. C. Chambers, and J. C. Burkhardt, *Higher Education for the Public Good.* San Francisco: Jossey-Bass, 2005.

Jacobs, F., and Hundley, S. P. "Can Attrition Be Controlled? Should Attrition Be Controlled? Interventions to Assist Students with Nontraditional Characteristics." *Metropolitan Universities,* 2005, *16*(2), 17–32.

Lewis, M. "Service Learning and Older Adults." *Educational Gerontology,* 2002, *28,* 655–667.

Market Wire. "University of Phoenix Selects VolunteerMatch to Promote Employee Volunteer Program." May 2007 (http://findarticles.com/p/articles/mi_pwwi/is_200705/ai_n19178766 (Retrieved October 20, 2007).

National Service-Learning Clearinghouse (NSLC). "Seniors and Youth Engaged in Service (SaYES)." Scotts Valley, Calif.: National Service-Learning Clearinghouse, 2006.

NSLC. "What Is Service-Learning? Service-Learning Is . . ." Scotts Valley, Calif.: National Service-Learning Clearinghouse, 2007 (http://servicelearning.org/what_is_service-learning/service-learning_is/index.php).

Points of Light Foundations (POLF). *Developing Excellence in Workplace Volunteer Programs: Guidelines for Success.* Washington, D.C.: Points of Light Foundation, 2004.

POLF. *The Promise Employee Skill-Based Volunteering Holds for Employee Skills and Nonprofit Sector Effectiveness.* Washington, D.C.: Points of Light Foundation, 2007.

New Directions for Adult and Continuing Education • DOI: 10.1002/ace

Prentice, M., and Robinson, G. "Service Learning and Civic Engagement in Community College Students." Paper presented at International Research Conference on Service-Learning and Community Engagement, Portland, Ore., Oct. 2006.
Prentice, M., and Robinson, G. *Linking Service Learning and Civic Engagement in Community College Students.* Washington, D.C.: American Association of Community Colleges, 2007 (www.aacc.nche.edu/servicelearning).
Robinson, G., and Barnett, L. *Service Learning and Community Colleges: Where We Are.* Washington, D.C.: AACC, 1996.
Robinson, G., and Henderson, E. "AACC Learn and Serve America Grant Program Evaluation Results." Unpublished manuscript. Washington, DC: AACC, 2000.
Tinto, V. *Leaving College: Rethinking the Cause and the Cures of Student Attrition.* Chicago: University of Chicago Press, 1999.
University of the Third Age. Retrieved Jan. 20, 2008, from http://www.u3a.org.uk.
Wilson, L. B., and Simson, S. P. (eds.). *Civic Engagement and the Baby Boomer Generation.* Binghamton, N.Y.: Haworth Press, 2006.
Yankelovich, D. "Ferment and Change: Higher Education in 2015." *Chronicle of Higher Education,* Nov. 25, 2005 (http://chronicle.com/weekly/v52/i14/14b00601.htm).

BARBARA HOLLAND is director of Learn and Serve America's National Service-Learning Clearinghouse, based at ETR Associates in Scotts Valley, Calif., and a senior scholar at Indiana University-Purdue University Indianapolis.

GAIL ROBINSON is manager of service learning at the American Association of Community Colleges in Washington, D.C.

3

Core professional values were fostered among adult social work students through structured reflection on their community based learning experiences.

Developing Professional Values: Campus and Community Perspectives on a Social Work Partnership

Rachael Richter-Hauk, Julie Arias

Licensed social work practice requires a willingness on the part of the practitioner to adhere to a professional values, knowledge, and skills base as reflected in the National Association of Social Workers' Code of Ethics (1996). Students who understand and aspire to this, and who gain experience interacting with people in a service capacity, will be able to make a more informed decision about their goodness of fit with the professional requirements of social work. The literature on adult learning reinforces service learning as an effective pedagogical approach to facilitate development of professional values. Experiential learning and reflection, two essential components of adult learning, are the essence of the service learning methodology. This chapter discusses how adult students in a social work program were supported in heightening and deepening their professional values through a successful service learning partnership between a faculty member at Capital University's Dayton Center and a practitioner with East End Community Services in Dayton, Ohio.

Note: We would like to thank the Capital University students, Mary Anne Cole, Mimi Johnson, and André Woods, for their enthusiasm for this project and their willingness to share their comments and feedback publicly. We would also like to thank Deborah Woods, who facilitated the focus group.

Literature Support for Fostering Professional Values Through Service Learning

Our decision to use service learning with adult students for the purpose of developing professional values is well supported by the literature. Our experience-based approach is congruent with adult learning theory, which suggests that adults place high value on being involved in learning and on incorporating prior knowledge and experience into the learning process (Caffarella and Barnett, 1994). More specifically, we draw on situated learning theory to teach professional values in an "authentic context" where a knowledge base is presented in concert with learning activities in the field (Brown, Collins, and Duguid, as cited in Cruess and Cruess, 2006, p. 205).

Others have found satisfying results from an authentic context approach. Williams and Reeves (2004) incorporated service learning into the Master in Social Work (MSW) program at the University of Georgia. Students reported that their weeklong experience at a burn camp for children enhanced development of their personal and professional self and their exploration of social work values. Social work students from the United States and Scotland who participated in a study abroad exchange program reported becoming more open-minded in their thinking and more aware of their own values as well as the values of the social work profession. They also reported developing an appreciation for cultural sensitivity and cultural competence, including enhanced awareness of issues of social justice (Lindsey, 2005).

These two studies illustrate how core values of social work—service, social justice, dignity and worth of the person, importance of human relationships, integrity, and competence (National Association of Social Workers, 1996)—can be elevated for students through service learning. The rest of this chapter focuses on our experience with fostering values of social work students through a service learning partnership.

Building a Successful Partnership Between Campus and Community

Our partnership began when Rachael, from Capital University, contacted Julie, a program facilitator at East End, to investigate possible community based learning opportunities for beginning social work students. Rachael had been using service learning in her classes for three years and received training on use of service learning pedagogy; Julie routinely worked each semester with service learning students from another local university. Julie identified a service gap at East End and suggested that the Capital University students could help with child care for the Milagro de Mujer program. This programming, which brings in speakers on topics of women's health, is an initiative targeted to the Latina/Hispanic immigrant community in Dayton, Ohio.

New Directions for Adult and Continuing Education • DOI: 10.1002/ace

We generated a written memo of understanding that clearly delineated the service learning objectives and areas of responsibility for faculty, students, and community partner. Our objectives were for students to enhance their professional values while offering culturally appropriate services to clients, working collaboratively with others, and demonstrating knowledge of social issues and service delivery. We agreed that in addition to site supervision Julie would be responsible for teaching the students about Latina immigrant culture, given her expertise in this area.

Preparing the Students

The students in the course were between the ages of forty and fifty-five. One man was African American and two women were Caucasian. All of the students had some prior experience working in a service agency.

We held an orientation session for the students at East End, which included a tour of the facility and discussion of the memo of understanding, available services, and cultural issues. The students also prepared reading materials about Latino culture, professional social work values, and principles of service learning. We coached the students on questions to ask the children that might help the students discover commonalities in the human experience and learn about the challenges the children face. We encouraged questions of this kind: "Can you tell me about your culture or your family's culture?" "What is it like to speak both English and Spanish?" "How do you help your parents with language difficulties?" "Do you like living in the United States?" Anticipating ways to engage with the children helped the students interact more easily with them once on site.

Student Service Activities

The cultural exchange began through play. The students developed creative activities and supplied materials to engage the children during weekly sessions. The students laid the foundation, and the children added their own flair. They played games, completed craft projects, walked to the park, talked, and listened. As part of their coursework, students compiled two binders full of craft and activity ideas from the Latino culture and tradition as well as games popularized in the United States. The students were able to secure donated materials for many of the activities and used them throughout the term.

The students were later invited to participate more deeply with the community by helping with two events that were organized and carried out by community members: the Mobile Mexican Consulate and the Appalachian Festival. During these events, the students organized volunteers, solicited community input for future programming, and participated in the activities. It was during these times that the students were more fully immersed in these diverse communities and experienced being the minority themselves.

Partners' Activities During the Service Period

Julie's interactions with the students centered on inviting and answering questions to heighten their cultural awareness and on highlighting ways in which their service enabled East End Community Services to fill a significant gap in services. Also during those discussions, some myths about immigration were debunked. As one student wrote in her final paper: "I was concerned about how some would just up and leave while we were here. We never did know why. . . . Some didn't have a choice—they had to leave and go back to their country." Another commented: "We certainly feel America is the greatest country—why would you want to leave? Obviously some feel differently." In addition, the students learned that language does not always have to be a barrier. Our project challenged mainstream perspectives that are often based on limited contact with minority communities. What better way to learn about a new community than through invested and reflective time spent with children?

Rachael's role was primarily to facilitate reflection and integration of the service experience with course reading material, including the NASW Code of Ethics (1996) and NASW Cultural Competence Standards for Practice (2001). Students reflected on their experiences in the classroom, at the agency, in online Blackboard discussions, and in written assignments. Specifically, students were asked to write about their actual experiences in the community and then to articulate their analysis, interpretation, and connection of these experiences to the course reading material. For example, after reading about some of the cultural characteristics of Latino families and engaging in the first child care session at East End, one student wrote, "The trust of family . . . was demonstrated when two boys realized they knew a cousin in common; it allowed an instant bond between them."

In addition, students were asked to write a paper integrating their service learning experience with the subject matter and stated objectives of the course.

Developing Professional Values

The primary sources of data for our qualitative analysis of the students' reflection activities were their written assignments and our focus group conversations. The results indicate that the project fostered growth and development of students' core professional values by giving them an opportunity for structured reflection and exploration of personal values and ethics through service experiences with diverse populations. For example, development of the NASW core professional value of service is illustrated by this student comment: "I had forgotten how a small group of dedicated and determined people could make a difference in the lives of the people they serve."

The core professional value of dignity and worth of the individual encourages respect for individual differences and cultural and ethnic diversity. In addition, social workers recognize the importance of human relationships as a core value. This student's reflection shows an understanding of these core values:

> One little girl named Ruth put everything in perspective for me. Ruth could talk but she mainly mumbled in Spanish. I rarely knew what she was saying yet we communicated what we needed to. If she fell down she came to me for comfort. If another child was annoying her she made me aware of it. She [would look] for me so that she could give me a hug for hello or goodbye. This made me realize that no matter what our situations were before we met, we learned to like and respect each other because of time well spent.

Similarly, student comments exemplified the development of cultural competence, and particularly understanding of the importance of cross-cultural knowledge and language diversity. One student noted, "Working with the community that East End serves has given me a much different perspective of the neighborhood and the Appalachian and Hispanic people who live within it." This student goes on to explain the rationale behind the group's choices about their final project:

> With our project we decided to honor their culture but also expose them to ours. We found a variety of games and crafts that were traditional Mexican and 100 percent American. We arranged to get books that dealt with the issues common to their neighborhood and culture [such as] . . . gangs, different ethnic groups, moving and changing schools. . . . We chose bilingual books to aid in that pesky task of reading they all disliked.

Conclusion

A number of key components contributed to our effective partnership: previously received training on service learning best practices, clearly stated objectives, effective communication, commitment to joint decision making, and use of a community partner as coeducator. As we reflected on the experience ourselves, we realized that these components are also supported by the literature (Bringle and Hatcher, 2002). It was particularly helpful to all involved to have a coeducator with thorough knowledge of the cultural group the students were serving.

This community-based learning experience at East End Community Services gave Capital University social work students the opportunity to participate in service delivery while reflecting on their level of commitment to professional social work values. The qualitative data, presented here in the form of student observations, support our conclusion that the students' professional values were enhanced through the service learning experience.

References

Bringle, R. G., and Hatcher, J. A. "Campus-Community Partnerships: The Terms of Engagement." *Journal of Social Issues,* 2002, *58*(3), 503–516.

Caffarella, R. S., and Barnett, B. G. "Characteristics of Adult Learners and Foundations of Experiential Learning." In L. Jackson and R. S. Caffarella (eds.), *Experiential Learning: A New Approach.* San Francisco: Jossey-Bass, 1994.

Cruess, R. L., and Cruess, S. R. "Teaching Professionalism: General Principles." *Medical Teacher,* 2006, *28*(3), 205–208.

Lindsey, E. W. "Study Abroad and Values Development in Social Work Students." *Journal of Social Work Education,* 2005, *41*(2), 229–249.

National Association of Social Workers (NASW). *NASW Code of Ethics.* Washington, D.C., 1996.

National Association of Social Workers (NASW). *NASW Cultural Competence Standards for Practice.* Washington, D.C., 2001.

Williams, N. R., and Reeves, P. M. "MSW Students Go to Burn Camp: Exploring Social Work Values Through Service-Learning." *Social Work Education,* 2004, *23*(4), 383–398.

RACHAEL RICHTER-HAUK received her MSW from Washington University. At the time this project was completed, she was assistant professor of social work at Capital University's Dayton Center for Lifelong Learning. Currently she is working in clinical practice.

JULIE ARIAS earned her bachelor's degree from Earlham College. Between 2003 and 2007, she worked at East End Community Services Corporation for the Milagro de Mujer program and also acted as the Latino/Hispanic family advocate. She is currently living in Ecuador.

New Directions for Adult and Continuing Education • DOI: 10.1002/ace

4

A new service learning program at a community college uses evaluation results to improve the experience for adult students.

Community Colleges and Adult Service Learners: Evaluating a First-Year Program to Improve Implementation

Liz Largent, Jon B. Horinek

Community colleges have been called the "people's college"; enrolling a diverse student population and serving their communities are both central to the roots and present-day mission of community colleges (Levinson, 2004). Nationwide, the demographic characteristics and associated challenges of community college students that Holland and Robinson explain in Chapter Two of this volume are very different from those found in four-year universities. A diverse student population consisting of students, who face financial, academic, and personal issues creates a unique challenge for community colleges to meet all students' needs. Despite the difficulty of meeting the needs of a diverse population, community colleges are in an ideal position to combat the public criticism that institutions of higher education are not responsive to societal problems, through use of community based educational programs (Hodge, Lewis, Kramer, and Hughes, 2001). In fact, development of service learning programs in community colleges has been increasing (Prentice, 2002).

The age, class, and racial and ethnic diversity of students must be considered in designing a service learning program in a community college. With respect to age variation, besides discrepancies in work schedules that can affect service learning programming, younger and older adults approach a community based project with varying levels of expertise and work

NEW DIRECTIONS FOR ADULT AND CONTINUING EDUCATION, no. 118, Summer 2008 © 2008 Wiley Periodicals, Inc.
Published online in Wiley InterScience (www.interscience.wiley.com) • DOI: 10.1002/ace.294

experience. Adults also have distinctive approaches to learning, as authors throughout this volume have discussed, that could affect the process of reflection as well. Fiddler and Marienau (Chapter Seven) point out that because all students bring prior experience to reflection, it is likely that adults will find the process of identifying their preconceptions particularly meaningful.

Building evaluation processes into a new program helps community college administrators ensure that they are meeting the diverse needs of their student population. When we conducted a study of a first-year program at a community college in the southwest, older students were found to be less satisfied with their experience, and so interviews were conducted to gain insight into why such a difference by age might exist. This allowed us to restructure our program to address the apparent concerns of adult service learners and increase satisfaction among service learners of all ages. This chapter discusses establishment of a service learning program in a community college, the results of a first-year evaluation, and subsequent redesign and evaluation.

Developing a Service Learning Program

With more than 80 percent of community colleges having developed a community based learning program, many have learned the importance of and challenges associated with implementing a strong, sustainable program. Prentice (2002) suggests a number of best practices for community colleges wishing to sustain long-term service learning programs. The most critical first step is to establish a center to oversee use of service learning across the curriculum. Next, it is important to include service learning in syllabi to reflect expectations and requirements. Training and recognition for students, faculty members, and community agency leaders is also critical. Faculty members using service learning as part of their curriculum should also be encouraged and given opportunities to collaborate. Finally, emphasis ought to be placed on using strong evaluative and assessment instruments to measure the success of the program and as a guide for future improvements.

Placing a service learning office in the college structure is a key factor in developing broad administrative support, from department chairs to deans to vice presidents across the institution (Robinson, 2000). Although the highest-quality service learning programs are collaborative efforts between academic and student affairs and draw on the expertise of both, the primary responsibility for service learning must be housed in one area or the other. Programs housed in student affairs are often student- and service-focused and can more easily adjust to address student needs. Depending on the culture of the institution, however, such programs may lack academic credibility and stable institutional funding. On the other hand, programs administered by academic affairs are often more strongly supported and deeply connected to the academic mission and allow students to better draw on course content. Programs housed in academic affairs may also place too little emphasis on service and be lacking in terms of adequate administrative policies and procedures (Jacoby, 1999). It is critical to establish a specific office to support faculty, students, and community partners engaged in service learning. Placement of such an office may depend on a number of institutional characteristics, notably funding, culture, and expertise.

First-Year Assessment

The service learning program being studied is in place at a large, single-campus, urban community college in the southwest with an annual enrollment of approximately nineteen thousand individual students. At the time of the study, the service learning program had completed its first year of implementation, with administrative responsibilities housed in student services. A total of fifteen courses formally incorporated service learning into the curriculum: ten in nursing, three in humanities courses, one in communication, and one in an occupational therapist assistant course. In the first year, 736 students participated in the program, completing 5,314 hours of service. In all fifteen courses, the service learning component was a mandatory assignment, with designated hours of service and a reflective writing assignment. Faculty members instructing each course worked with student service administrators to include service learning in their curriculum. Each faculty member submitted specific learning objectives for the course, linked to service learning, and selected appropriate service agencies from which students could select one to complete their assignment.

Forty-seven agencies were available from which to choose. Representatives from each agency completed an initial intake form to be considered a "partner agency." Representatives were sent training materials and also invited for one-hour training sessions at the beginning of the fall and spring semesters. After selection by a faculty member, each agency representative was sent the learning objectives associated with the course for which he or she had been selected. In some cases, one agency was selected for multiple courses. To serve as a partner agency, each had to meet the criteria of (1) being a nonprofit organization or one that supplies needed service to the community, (2) offering continuous volunteer opportunities, (3) having a designated volunteer coordinator, (4) operating within a radius of approximately fifty miles of the campus, and (5) attending the agency orientation or scheduling an individual meeting with service learning administrators.

As part of the course evaluation process, students who were enrolled in a course with a service learning component were asked to complete a survey with eight satisfaction-related questions and two open-ended questions. Of the 736 students enrolled in a course with a service learning component during the fall and spring semesters, 475 completed the survey. Of those surveyed, 82 percent were female, 15 percent were male, 0.2 percent were transgender, and 3 percent did not respond. Concerning ethnicity,

New Directions for Adult and Continuing Education • DOI: 10.1002/ace

Table 4.1. Satisfaction Survey Means

Question	Mean
The service increased my awareness of the larger community.	3.96
The service helped me better understand community needs.	3.97
The service helped me reflect on my life and goals.	3.49
The service helped me decide on career and life goals.	2.84
The service has increased my interest in doing further service.	3.60
I would recommend this activity to my friends.	3.62
My experience with the community agency was positive.	4.23
My experience with the Service-Learning program has been positive.	4.04

8 percent were Black, 4 percent American Indian or Alaskan, 4 percent Asian, 4 percent Latino, 68 percent white, 0.4 percent Native Hawaiian/Pacific Islander, 2 percent other, and 9 percent not responding. Of those participating, 64 percent indicated that neither parent had attended college or earned a bachelor's degree. Regarding age, 15 percent were between eighteen and twenty-two, 37 percent were between twenty-three and thirty, 42 percent were thirty-one or older, and 6 percent did not respond.

The eight satisfaction questions were built on a five-point Likert-type scale, from strongly disagree to strongly agree, with no specific neutral. Means on each question are listed above in Table 4.1.

One-way analysis of variance using Tukey's post hoc test was performed on each demographic characteristic and responses to each of the eight questions to ensure the service learning experience was addressing the needs of a diverse student population. No significant difference was found on any of the eight questions ($p > .05$) as correlated to demographic characteristics, with the exception of age. For age, on all questions except for the one regarding whether or not they would recommend the service learning activity to a friend, there were significant differences ($p < .05$) among the three age ranges identified just above. Overall, students in the eighteen-to-twenty-two age range tended to show a higher level of satisfaction than those twenty-three and older.

To better understand why nontraditional students may be less satisfied with academic service learning than their younger counterparts, qualitative interviews were conducted with some students age twenty-three and older. Students were randomly selected, contacted by telephone, and asked to participate. The four interview participants were female, over the age of twenty-four, and married. Two participants indicated overall satisfaction with their service learning experience, but two others were dissatisfied. These four interviews raised two issues that were used to improve students' experiences in the service learning program: first, adult students need work tasks that are clearly meaningful; and second, they need to relate prior experience to their work in the community.

New Directions for Adult and Continuing Education • DOI: 10.1002/ace

In assessing their experiences in the community, all four students discussed the significance to themselves and the community of the activities they were assigned as well as the importance of regular interaction with and involvement in the work of the staff. Those who did not enjoy the experience did not perceive that there was enough work to be done and did not believe their work benefited the mission of the agency. On the other hand, those who enjoyed their experience were able to more clearly articulate how the work they had done had contributed to helping others.

One dissatisfied student selected a clinic to complete her service, because she believed it would be related to her academic major, nursing. In reflecting on her experience, the student stated:

> . . . They were like, 'Oh well I guess we have a little bit of filing if you want to put some packets together or something.' I wish it was more, this is what we do. And at this particular clinic I mean they did well-baby visits and labs and things of that nature. It would have been nice to at least been able to observe that for me personally.

Both dissatisfied students indicated that when working at their respective agencies they were relatively isolated from others at the agency, which seemed to further their frustration and feelings that the work they were doing had little connection to the mission of the agency or their coursework.

On the other hand, during an interview with someone who had a positive experience at the agency she had selected, one student's sense of accomplishment and belief that she had made a difference shined through. The student explained: "I help them. Some of the residents were not, you know, able to write, so I helped them to write. I helped with lunch, I cleaned around after we finished eating, I helped feed those that couldn't feed themselves. . . . It was fun actually."

Unlike both the students who were dissatisfied, the satisfied students had more contact with clients and agency representatives during their experience and were given an array of tasks to complete. It is also important to note that, in the case of the satisfied students, agency representatives took time to explain their mission and the basic work they performed. The lack or benefit of such agency background information seemed to affect participants' satisfaction, and we resolved to use this information in redesigning our program.

Not only did both dissatisfied students not understand the purpose of the assignment, but they also found the assignment devaluing their life experience. One student expressed her belief that she should not be required to complete service hours because she had life experience that had already taught her what she needed to know:

> I think people who have life experience, I mean, it's not fair to limit it to an age group or to people who still live with mommy and daddy, or who just

moved out. But, if you're married and you have children, at some point and time you've actually done service or helped with something, with somebody. I think that should count, your life experience, you should have to document it.

It could be concluded from this comment that adult students who have prior experience with service activities see a service learning requirement as redundant. We conclude instead that this valuable previous knowledge and experience should be incorporated in the reflection process so that prior and current learning are better integrated.

Program Redesign

During the first two semesters of operation of the service learning program, decisions about reflection, training, course objectives, and agency choice were largely left to the faculty members. Administrators from the service learning program initially felt that interference with the work of the faculty members might be viewed negatively by participating instructors. From the findings from the first assessment effort, however, it became clear that more training and oversight was needed if faculty, students, and volunteer agencies were to improve reflection exercises to draw on students' prior experience and improve service project objectives in order to make the service more meaningful for students.

Improving Reflection to Draw on Prior Experience

Administrators first focused attention on faculty participating in the service learning program. Comments and observations from faculty members confirmed the findings of both the quantitative and the qualitative research conducted by the program. Faculty members observed that students from older age groups were, in large part, not making connections among their coursework, life experiences, and the service learning assignment. After meeting with faculty individually, we saw clearly that they desired training on how to encourage in-class reflection with students.

The service learning program initially gave faculty ways to assess and conduct summative reflection exercises. However, little information was previously available for ongoing reflection, which adult learning research has shown is crucial for adult students to connect their out-of-class experiences with in-class material (see Marienau and Reed, Chapter Six of this volume). As a result of feedback from faculty members and data collected from students, service learning administrators conducted an intensive training session designed to give instructors the tools necessary to foster ongoing and relevant reflection, rather than focusing solely on the summative reflection assignment, as well as additional guidance on use of self-directed learning theory.

New Directions for Adult and Continuing Education • DOI: 10.1002/ace

During the faculty training session, administrators reviewed three primary topics. First, findings from the quantitative and qualitative data were shared with instructors so they could gain insight and clarity regarding student perceptions of the service learning program. Next, the importance of reflection was discussed, emphasizing that it was consistent, continuous, and connected (Eyler and Giles, 1999). Reflection must be positive and combat negative perceptions of service learning; it must be done before, during, and after the service experience, and it must aid students in making connections to their life experience and course content. Faculty members were also given reflection exercises and discussion topics to aid them in facilitating consistent, continuous, and connected reflection. Instructors were given five-minute discussion topics that could be used throughout the academic semester, as well as a number of creative postreflection ideas. During the first year of the service project, all faculty members used a summative paper as the postreflection exercise that was frequently regarded negatively by students. As a result, instructors were introduced to alternative postreflection exercises such as video productions, project displays, presentations, skits, and art projects, all of which could be done individually or in groups. Finally, administrators engaged faculty members in discussion of self-directed learning theory. Emphasis was placed on how the service learning experience was very different from course assignments in that students were being asked to take responsibility for their own learning, ask questions, and engage fully in the experience. Given that most instruction and assignments adhere to a more traditional pedagogy, care needed to be given to aid students in approaching the service learning experience as a self-directed learner.

Improving Goal Setting to Make Service More Meaningful

To aid in making the service experience more meaningful, administrators expanded their initial classroom visit to include a prereflection exercise and focused on training for agency representatives. During the first year of the program, representatives from the service learning center were invited into class periods to explain the service learning process. Administrators took this time to go over rules and regulations, expectations, agency choice, timesheet procedures, and liability concerns. After the research was conducted, it became clear that this procedure needed to be enhanced and expanded. An empirical study of youths engaged in service learning suggests that students who value service and have an emotional investment in the cause or issue represented by the agency report more positive gains from the activity, including increased social responsibility and community belonging (McGuire and Gamble, 2006). This study of adults in higher education suggests that despite a student's investment in the agency mission, as was the case with the student who completed the service in the clinic, the student's expectations of the experience might not be met. Although not directly stated in the data, it may be reasonable to assert that in the phenomenon presented the dissatisfaction was more closely related to the students' expectations of what tasks would be performed during the service than to the cause being served. That is, students may expect to have a direct or obvious impact at the agency. It may be that more contact with agency clients or clearer explanation of the value of the tasks being performed could aid in the students feeling as though their efforts were meaningful.

In addition to reviewing procedures and policies, administrators now conduct an opening reflection exercise with students in the classroom to help frame the service learning assignment in a way that is more obviously connected to the course material and prior experience. Additionally, students are given more information about the assignment before the semester begins. During this orientation, a guide is distributed to students that outlines detailed learning objectives for the assignment, how those learning objectives would be assessed, suggestions for a good experience and a realistic view of what the students should expect in completing the required service, results from the previous evaluation surveys, and positive student comments.

An expanded agency listing supplemented these efforts by including more information about what potential volunteers would experience at the service site. The listing also addressed expected time commitments and training at the individual agencies. Administrators began sending biweekly e-mail reminders to faculty with tips on how to integrate reflection into their class period.

The research conducted during the first year of the program not only exposed areas for improvement in the classroom but also suggested ways to enhance the experience for students at the service sites. Prior to the study, participating partner agencies were required to attend an agency orientation program before receiving service learning volunteers. Introductory in nature, this program was designed to simply explain the program's rules and regulations to volunteer administrators. After the study, the program was expanded to include demographic information about the students, how best to use them in a volunteer setting, and how to enhance their experience to encourage repeat volunteer participation.

The session was titled "Recruiting and Retaining Service Learning Volunteers" and focused on giving volunteer administrators practical advice on how to interact and engage service learning volunteers as well as volunteers from the general population. This presentation included information on recruiting and retaining volunteers, national trends in volunteer participation with agency representatives, what to expect with the institution's service learning students, and a service learning program overview.

In the next session, participants were given demographic information about the service learning volunteers. This included results from the first study and suggestions on helping students, specifically adult students, gain value from their experiences. The suggestions:

• *Design projects for a shorter span of time and encourage volunteers to work in groups.* Students consistently cited lack of time and flexibility as one of their frustrations with the assignment. If agencies are more sensitive to this fact and design shorter projects, students could more easily fit service into their schedule. This effort is also overtly conscious of students' life circumstances and commitments beyond college, another frustration expressed in research.

• *Communicate with volunteers by explaining how the students' work is contributing to the organization.* Some students expressed the belief that the work they were doing was meaningless and added little value to the organization. Agencies were encouraged to communicate with volunteers and present concrete examples of how their work is vital to the agency's goals, and most important to the people being served.

• *Be sensitive about assigning tasks by working to understand what interests the student.* All students come to service learning with learning goals that can be taken into consideration in choosing their activities at the site. Adults are likely to have expertise as well that would benefit the organization and elicit satisfaction for the student. It is important to encourage agencies to remain cognizant of students' lives and interests and consequently give students needed recognition and understanding.

• *Do not leave the volunteer alone.* Although simple, this suggestion seemed to have the most relevance with students. Students responded better to the service when they were included as part of the office staff at the volunteer agency. Such interaction enhances learning and offers clearer understanding of the organization's mission.

• *Make training meaningful.* Students consistently viewed training as a meaningless part of their service experience. Agencies should recognize that some students have the skills they are looking for because of work experience. Assessing those skills can allow agencies to offer training on issues such as the cultural differences that students may encounter working in the community.

All of these efforts were made in direct response to our assessment of the service learning program's first year. Participants cited time and multiple competing priorities as sources of dissatisfaction with the service learning experience, in addition to perceived lack of meaningfulness in their work and the desire to have their knowledge and experience recognized. Therefore, we asked faculty members using service learning in the classroom to remain cognizant of these pitfalls and seek methods of including the student's previous experience into the reflection exercise, offering upfront understanding of the learning outcomes and clear shows of support.

Community agencies were encouraged to recognize adult expertise in planning activities and interact with them throughout their involvement to ensure a more meaningful experience for students.

Follow-up Assessment Results

The satisfaction survey was administered to students again following implementation of practical enhancements to the service learning program. The survey instrument contained eight satisfaction-related questions and two open-ended questions. The eight satisfaction questions were built on a five-point Likert-type scale from strongly disagree to strongly agree, with no specific neutral.

One-way analysis of variance using Tukey's post hoc test was performed on each demographic characteristic and responses to each of the eight questions to ensure the service learning experience was now meeting the needs of a diverse student population. No significant difference was found on any of the eight questions ($p > .05$) as correlated to demographic characteristics. Thus age was no longer a factor in the extent to which students were satisfied with their experience. It is also important to note that the mean satisfaction on all eight Likert-type scale questions increased compared to data from the previous year.

Conclusion and Lessons Learned

Evaluation of a first-year service learning program in a community college with a diverse population raised important concerns about the effect of program design on adult students' satisfaction. Previous research on service learning participation in various higher education environments indicates that time, family, job responsibilities, insufficient clarity regarding the purpose of the activity, and lack of enthusiasm on the part of instructors are all cited as reasons for dissatisfaction or lack of engagement in service learning (Hughes, 2002; Fertman, 1993). This study reinforces and expands these findings. Participants cited time and multiple competing priorities as a source of dissatisfaction with the service learning experience, and interviews with adult students helped to identify areas in which the program could be modified.

Specifically, care ought to be given to placing value on the students' life experiences. As with any form of education, offering opportunities for learners to bring their own experience into the project will likely make for a more meaningful and holistic service learning experience. In addition, care should be given to the agencies selected for use in a service learning program as well as the expectations students have for a service experience. Although not all service is as interactive as students may expect, it is important that the agencies selected have meaningful opportunities for students to engage in; that agency staff be made aware of the learning objectives associated with the course for which the students are completing the service; and that an explanation of the connection between service tasks and agency mission be given to students before they begin engaging in the experience. There is little question regarding the positive benefits of service learning in the curriculum, but care must be given to its implementation.

Meeting the needs of a diverse student population can pose a number of challenges for educators and administrators. The improvements in reflection discussed here were good for all students involved, but adult students seemed to demand the changes because they need to have more understanding of what is expected, more attention to the need for their learning to be meaningful, and more connection to life experiences and control over their own learning. Community college administrators, faculty, and agency staff can offer a meaningful service learning experience for adults by taking these needs into consideration.

References

Eyler, J., and Giles, D. *Where's the Learning in Service-Learning?* San Francisco: Jossey-Bass, 1999.

Fertman, C. "The Pennsylvania Serve-America Grant: Implementation and Impact." Report no. BBB31285. Pittsburgh: Pennsylvania Service-Learning Resource and Evaluation Network, 1993. (ED 362 693)

Hodge, G., Lewis, T., Kramer, K., and Hughes, R. "Collaboration for Excellence: Engaged Scholarship at Collin County Community College." *Community College Journal of Research and Practice,* 2001, *25*(9), 675–690.

Hughes, A. "A Study of Service-Learning at Virginia Highlands Community College and Mountain Empire Community College." Unpublished doctoral dissertation, East Tennessee State University, 2002.

Jacoby, B. *Partnerships for Service-Learning.* New Directions for Student Services, no. 87. San Francisco: Jossey-Bass, 1999.

Levinson, D. L. "Introduction to the Special Issue on Community Colleges as Civic Institutions." *Community College Journal of Research and Practice,* 2004, *28*, 99–103.

McGuire, J. K., and Gamble, W. C. "Community Service for Youth: The Value of Psychological Engagement over Number of Hours Spent. *Journal of Adolescence,* 2006, *29*(2), 289–298.

Prentice, M. "Institutionalizing Service Learning in Community Colleges." *Horizons Research Brief for the American Association of Community Colleges.* Washington, D.C.: Community College Press, 2002.

Robinson, G. *Creating Sustainable Service Learning Programs: Lessons Learned from the Horizons Project, 1997–2000.* (Report from Corporation for National Service.) Annapolis Junction, Md.: Community Colleges Press, 2000.

Liz Largent is the dean of student development at Oklahoma City Community College. She is currently pursuing a Ph.D. in adult and higher education from the University of Oklahoma.

Jon B. Horinek is service learning and student life coordinator at Oklahoma City Community College. He is currently pursuing a Ph.D. in psychology.

Volunteers develop instrumental and interpersonal skills through their work with community organizations, a form of learning that could be deepened and expanded with intentional reflection.

Community Based Learning and Civic Engagement: Informal Learning among Adult Volunteers in Community Organizations

Karsten Mündel, Daniel Schugurensky

Many iterations of community based learning employ models, such as consciousness raising groups (Miles, 1996), cultural circles (Freire, 1970), and participatory action research (Hall, 1981). In all of them, learning is a deliberate part of an explicit educational activity. In this chapter, we explore another realm of community learning: the informal learning that results from volunteering in community based organizations. This is a relevant issue, because millions of adults play an active role all over the world in improving their communities through volunteer organizations (Salamon, 1999). When speaking to volunteers, one sees clearly that significant learning results from the unpaid work they engage in to improve their communities. In recent years, an emerging body of literature is exploring informal learning in social action and in social movements (see, for example, Finger, 1989; Ross-Gordon and Dowling, 1995; Belenky, Bond, and Weinstock,

Acknowledgments: We are thankful for the active participation of both the Cooperative Housing Federation of Toronto (CHFT) and the Ontario Healthy Communities Coalition (OHCC) in designing and implementing this research. Many of their members were also interviewed as part of our study. Further, we wish to acknowledge the work of Fiona Duguid and Jorge Sousa, who both participated in the Cooperative Housing study. We also thank the Social Science and Humanities Research Council of Canada (SSHRC) for funding this study.

1997; Kilgore, 1999; Foley, 1999; Eraut 2000; MacPherson, 2002; Colley, Hodkinson, and Malcom, 2004; and Hall, 2006).

In this chapter, we briefly put the concepts of informal learning and learning through volunteering into context. Then we explore three key areas in which volunteers learn: instrumental skills related to their organization, learning to work with others, and learning about the role of volunteering in society. We hope that by highlighting the breadth and depth of volunteers' learning we can encourage individual volunteers, and organizations working with volunteers, to focus more attention on the learning dimensions of this type of civic engagement. Along with our collaborators (see acknowledgments), we have researched volunteers' informal learning in a variety of settings. This study of volunteers' informal learning is part of the Work and Lifelong Learning Network, which involved twelve case studies and a national survey of the Canadian adult population on informal learning more generally (Livingstone and Scholtz, 2006). The information presented in this chapter draws mainly on two of our case studies, one with volunteers on housing cooperative committees and boards, and the other with volunteers in a variety of community based organizations. In these two case studies we interviewed eighty-two people (fifty-three women and twenty-nine men).

Informal Learning and Volunteering in Context

Because we are exploring the informal learning of volunteers, it is pertinent to start with a brief discussion of both informal learning and volunteer work. A common typology of educational activities distinguishes three subsystems: formal, nonformal, and informal. Formal education refers to the highly institutionalized, curricular-based instruction that takes place in schools and postsecondary institutions. Nonformal education refers to the realm of workshops and short educational sessions where learning is a recognized outcome of the activity. Informal learning is usually conceptualized as a residual category for all other learning activities, to include self-directed learning, incidental learning, and socialization (Schugurensky, 2000). Self-directed learning is intentional and conscious; incidental learning is unintentional but conscious; learning acquired through socialization (usually values, attitudes, and dispositions) is often unintentional and unconscious.

Most of the significant learning acquired throughout life is part of the informal subsystem. Pioneering educators such as Dewey (1916), Lindeman (1926), and Coady (1939) realized that informal learning in nonauthoritarian community environments nurtures associative intelligence to better understand and transform reality. In spite of its significant role in our lives, a great deal of informal learning is invisible and results in tacit knowledge, which Polanyi (1966) defined as "we know more than we can tell" (p. 4). This is largely because informal learning is acquired through activities such as volunteering that are not commonly thought to be educational. Just as this presented us as researchers with the challenge of eliciting informal

New Directions for Adult and Continuing Education • DOI: 10.1002/ace

learning from volunteers, it also presents a challenge to volunteers and volunteers' organizations to benefit from this largely unacknowledged learning. Although most people do not conceive community engagement through volunteering as a learning activity, our study suggests that relevant learning takes place in these settings. Through volunteers' engagement they acquire a range of skills, knowledge, attitudes, and values; such learning is often unintentional and unconscious.

Volunteer work is traditionally understood as work that is unpaid, freely chosen, and of benefit to society. In a recent survey (Hall, 2006), it was found that almost twelve million Canadians (45 percent of the population age fifteen and older) volunteered through an organization, and that their contribution totals almost two billion hours, an amount equivalent to one million full-time jobs. Additionally, 83 percent of Canadians reported volunteering on their own, without being part of an organization. The most frequent motivation for volunteering is the possibility of making a contribution to the community. Among other reasons are the opportunity to use one's skills and experience and being personally affected by the cause supported by the organization.

Given this context, we understand volunteering as a form of community engagement, and throughout this chapter we use the two terms interchangeably. Though there are differing types of volunteer work (Mündel and Schugurensky, 2005; Schugurensky, Mündel, and Duguid, 2006), it is important to note that the world of volunteering is changing, particularly as the state continues to download its responsibilities onto voluntary organizations (Blackstone, 2004; Bloom and Kilgore, 2003; Handy and others, 2000; Macduff, 2005). Here we address some of the informal learning of volunteers related to these changes and its relevance to voluntary organizations.

What is the relevance of examining the learning dimension of community engagement? Most people involved in their community commit a significant amount of time to, and in many cases have part of their identity tied up in, the amount of work they do in the community. In volunteer circles, there are recurrent references to the "eighty-twenty rule," to suggest that 20 percent of volunteers do approximately 80 percent of the work. This perception is based on reality, as confirmed by the findings from two recent studies of Canadian volunteering (Hall, Lasby, Gumulka, and Tryon, 2006; Hall, McKeown, and Roberts, 2001). Conceptualizing volunteering activities as doing *and* learning underscores the importance of this engagement to both the communities and the individuals involved. It also can point us to key things that community based organizations and the state can do to support those learning activities.

Learning from Civic Engagement

We found an amazing breadth and depth of learning resulting from the many forms of civic engagement. Interestingly, the types of learning were

New Directions for Adult and Continuing Education • DOI: 10.1002/ace

quite similar across case studies. To organize our findings, we arranged them into three key areas. First, most research participants indicated they had done significant instrumental learning of the skills and knowledge related to their particular type of engagement. Second, community engagement generated a great deal of interpersonal learning, which encompasses skills, knowledge, and dispositions about how to work and live together. Finally, we found there were many instances of learning through formal and informal reflection. This mode of learning is seen as particularly important for community organizations.

Instrumental Learning

Not surprisingly, a great amount of adults' learning was instrumental in the sense of being necessary to carry out a specific task. This learning ranged from skills such as learning to make coffee in a percolator and not having it taste like battery acid to how to prepare a budget for an organization's grant application. It also includes knowledge acquisition related to the mission of their particular organization, such as specific legislation on eviction or pollution.

For the most part, the instrumental learning related to skills— especially the routine ones related to specific computer software or working a photocopier—were implicit and resulted in tacit knowledge. That is, until we asked about specific skills, most volunteers did not list them as specific learning from their volunteering. There are instances where it is preferable for learning to remain tacit, as in the case of routine tasks carried out frequently. As Eraut (2000) notes, the use of tacit knowledge in routine action is a very efficient way of translating learning into action. This is the case in routine activities, but we argue that it is not the case in terms of dispositional or philosophical learning. We found that the greater the complexity of the skill, the greater the degree of volunteers' explicit knowledge about the learning. For instance, participants in both organizations consistently mentioned acquisition of computer-related skills. Computers seem to be part and parcel of the daily practices of most forms of community engagement. When asked about this, one housing co-op volunteer noted, "I had never used a computer until I came here. I got to use it in the housing co-op because everything had to be in writing before you could say something and it would be accepted."

At the level of skills (as different from knowledge-related instrumental learning), participants engaged in the community did not tend to undertake any deliberate or incidental reflective exercise in order to learn. The predominant learning modality was "learning by doing," with little consciousness of the act of cognition or learning. As we move to the more knowledge-based learning in this category, a greater degree of reflection started to take place. However, in many cases there was still little reflective activity, and what did occur was often quite incidental.

New Directions for Adult and Continuing Education • DOI: 10.1002/ace

At this point, it is pertinent to note that in the real world most learning is not either implicit or explicit; nor is it the result of only personal experience or acquisition of purely codified knowledge (Eraut, 2000). These categories are useful for analytical purposes, but in real life learning draws on numerous sources and consists in complex dynamics that are very difficult to dissect. As a woman who has volunteered with a sexual assault center explained, the hands-on experience of volunteering made her learning of codified knowledge at university more real and useful: "In the work that I've done with women's organizations over the years, I've deepened my knowledge around the issues of violence against women and children. I already had some knowledge from my studies but the work really helped me to understand that knowledge in a more practical way."

This volunteer has not only integrated different forms of knowledge but also developed significant knowledge about the issues related to the mission of her community based organization. Another important instrumental learning mentioned by participants related to managerial skills, particularly among those who have occupied leadership positions.

Learning to Work Together

We as researchers like developing categories into which to place our data, but the real lives of our research participants do not fit cleanly into our categories. Here is a quotation in which we see how a co-op board member has learned both management skills as well as more intangible "people skills": "Most people who come to the co-op have never been managers before, have never fired or hired staff, never been involved in repairs, etc. They don't have the people skills to be an employer. It is a great learning curve for everyone."

Indeed, people skills were an important area of learning for many volunteers, board members, and community activists. In fact, our data suggest that this is the area with the largest overlap between the case studies. The learning in this category includes not only skills such as making a list of speakers to ensure that everyone can participate or knowledge of decision-making processes but also dispositional learning such as openness toward people with diverse ideas and backgrounds. Although the majority of the learning in this category was the result of learning by doing, in the case of community based organizations as well as the housing cooperatives there were some nonformal educational activities, such as workshops and conferences, that offered volunteers important learning opportunities. Some also referred to the importance of training and other manuals for acquisition of skills, knowledge, and dispositions.

As this housing co-op volunteer noted, consensus building when people have different backgrounds is a real skill, which she acquired through her participation on the board: "Prior to living in the housing co-op, there wasn't much need for consensus building. As an activist in an activist group we were already all on the same side. We didn't need to build consensus really."

This quote deals with skill learning, but it is also clear that the participant developed a significant knowledge base about issues related to housing co-ops, which she puts into play when she uses her soft skills or decision-making skills. Because the reflective processes that lead to most of this learning were predominantly incidental and not a planned part of people's regular activities in their communities, we also identified some participants who learned that group decisions take too long ("Process takes too much time, and we need to act") or that some members are not willing to contribute their share ("You can't count on others to get the job done"). This, to many, would be seen as "destructive" learning in that it does not strengthen the organization people are volunteering in. However, most participants mentioned "constructive" learning, noting that group decision making is often time-consuming but is more rewarding, democratic, and effective in the long run. This confirms that people who have the same experience do not necessarily arrive at the same conclusions, but intentional processes of collective critical reflection can generate new learning by bringing together several perspectives on a particular issue, and perhaps come to an agreement on which decisions require collective democratic decision making and which executive decisions could be made by a small committee.

A few of the people we interviewed noted that during their volunteer experience they learned something about the particularities of certain groups. Some volunteers reported that the new learning confirmed their prior perceptions about a given group. By generalizing from an experience with one or two people to an entire community, there was a high probability that these volunteers were simply perpetuating their stereotypes about a particular group (Allport, 1954). In other cases, the opposite process took place. This happened, for instance, when the social interactions of the volunteer experience helped individuals disconfirm their own prejudices and challenge their stereotypes. For instance, one immigrant woman who volunteers in the housing cooperative noted that she had negative prejudice toward homosexuals, but that after regular interactions in the committee work she experienced a significant attitudinal change: "In Latin America we are very closed about sexual orientation and it [the committee] was the first time that I started to interact with gays and lesbians and to understand them for what they are, and to look at them as human beings. I opened my mind. In my country we close the doors to them."

A participant who, at the time of the interview, did volunteer work with more than ten organizations experienced a similar dispositional change. She noted that the new interactions helped her challenge some prior learning acquired in early socialization: "I was raised Salvation Army. Volunteering opened my eyes to a new way of thinking about people's sexuality. . . . Even acceptance has that hint, respect, not just tolerance. I don't think 'Just tolerate.' They are just the same as I am; no difference except in their sexual orientation. People are people!"

These two examples exhibit what Mezirow (2000) calls transformative learning. In part through community engagement, these individuals have undergone a major shift in their frames of reference changing how they interact, in this case, with people of differing sexual orientation.

For some volunteers, the shift in frames of reference led to new ways of interacting with individuals who are different from them. For others, it led to a shift in how they look at society in general. "[My organization] has taught me to work from an ideology that people want authenticity in their relationships, and to break down the structures separating us from one another. It's also helping me to know how to heal ways in which we've been hurt. For example, it helped to address the impacts that internalized oppression has on all our groups. It also helped me to work on my assumptions about other groups."

In the case of these adults, as in other cases of transformative learning examined by Mezirow and associates (2000), shifts in frames of reference involved experiencing a disorienting dilemma, engaging in a critical assessment of one's assumptions, exploring new roles and relationships, building confidence in those new roles and relationships, and reintegrating one's life experiences into the new perspective.

Learning About the Role and Importance of Volunteering

In this category, we include learning about engaging in community itself, especially how volunteering and the voluntary sector fit into the overall political economy. Even though the majority of research participants did not engage in this type of learning, it is indicative of the progressive potential of learning from community engagement. Within all these case studies, some of the participants are aware of the regressive elements of their community engagement, such as filling a gap that has grown on account of state downloading to the nonprofit sector (see, for example, Bloom and Kilgore, 2003; Lacey and Ilcan, 2006; Mitchell, 2001).

Of the three categories we have developed, learning in this category cannot really be implicit. The amount of consideration necessary to be reflexive about the volunteering activity implies a certain degree of explicit learning. Interestingly, as a result of the advocacy work of the Cooperative Housing Federation of Toronto, most of the housing co-op volunteers were able to speak against the negative effects of "the download"—shifting responsibility for housing to the municipal level on the part of both federal and provincial governments. Volunteers' awareness of this negative trend was the result of reflective as well as informational sessions in which representatives from the municipal, provincial, and national arms of the cooperative housing movement met with co-op boards and volunteers to discuss impending cuts and downloading of responsibility. Many volunteers spoke about the download; many fewer spoke about development of political efficacy beyond the housing co-operative in spite of specific questions attempting to elicit volunteers' learning on this topic.

Most of the volunteers could articulate their learning relative to making changes in their co-op (especially those who had served their cooperative at both committee and board levels) but far fewer could articulate how to make changes to policy at the municipal, provincial, or federal level. Other volunteers, however, developed greater political efficacy (that is, the confidence that they can influence the political system) through their participation in co-op governance: ". . . The biggest thing that I learned was that there is nothing to be afraid of. You may have to go after them a few times, whether it is the politicians or your own board of directors. But you keep hammering away and eventually they get tired of doing it and they are going to start listening to you . . . or they will call Security!"

A second quote specifically shows how this same co-op board member has transferred her learning from the housing co-op context of a minidemocracy to the larger political process at the federal level, and it suggests the importance of reflective activities in developing consciousness:

> . . . Even as an entire group we aren't on our own. We have to think of bigger and bigger communities. How do we take what [our] co-op is doing and apply that to what St. Lawrence neighborhood is doing, and apply that to Toronto, to Ontario, to Canada? But at the same time we also learn how we can help ourselves because of what these other parts of communities are doing. It's a back-and-forth thing.

This volunteer also told us that the various reflective activities were important ways in which she learned: talking with other volunteers, debriefing sessions of the board, and the annual national cooperative housing movement conference. Only the board debriefing sessions are formally planned, and even those were often scheduled in an ad hoc manner as the need arose. An interesting case is the national conference because by virtue of the fact that it brings together housing co-op members from across the country it creates spaces for the informal reflective activities of its members. Further, the issue that elicited this particular volunteer's comments was hearing about the problems facing housing cooperatives in British Columbia. That is, reflection on the relationship between her experience with self-governance in her co-op and the federal democratic process grew indirectly out of a session planned at the national meeting.

Aside from the non-formal educational experiences of the conference and the occasional board debriefing, there were generally no formal opportunities for this type of reflective activity. This is a relevant issue, because even when this volunteer learned about citizenship in a predominantly informal mode, it was still the result of a series of deliberately educational

New Directions for Adult and Continuing Education • DOI: 10.1002/ace

activities. In this regard, we argue that community organizations should offer more spaces that encourage cross-fertilization of nonformal and informal learning that could lead to a higher level of understanding and commitment to the organization.

In both organizations that participated in this study, there were generally no formal opportunities for this type of reflexive activity. These two groups of volunteers mentioned they never had the time to really stop and take a break, and paid employees in the organization often did not have time to answer their questions. In this context, it is easy to see why an organization that depends on volunteers to carry out its mandate may not want to engage in critical reflection about its role in delivering public services. Such reflection may lead to increasing awareness of the regressive elements of all this volunteer activity and thereby decrease volunteers' motivation to be active. Volunteer organizations are often in a very difficult situation if they are supplying important public services, knowing that if they do not find a way to deliver the service then it will likely not happen. This can help justify decisions vis-à-vis state funding and other management approaches that have a significant negative impact on the expectations placed on volunteers and the voluntary organization as a whole.

Several of the community based volunteers were very articulate about their frustration with the state's downloading of responsibility onto volunteers. As one remarked, "If you prove you can do a good job, and you care about your objectives, other organizations in the government and private sector will try to take advantage of that to offload what should be paid work to nonprofit organizations."

Likewise, another volunteer pointed out that . . . "the regrettable fact is that the neoconservative trend in the management of federal, provincial, and municipal economies has covertly downloaded many of the services previously provided from tax revenues by civil servants or social service contractors to the volunteer sector."

Both of these quotations show the volunteers' awareness of the regressive potential of volunteer organizations' work. They are still contributing actively to their community, but they are increasingly playing roles previously taken on by the state. Theirs is not a call to stop volunteering or stop contributing as active, critical, and informed citizens, but rather to make sure their volunteer work is done in the name of making their community a better place—and not done in vain.

Summary, Conclusions, and Recommendations

In this study, we found that people who are engaged in community organizations acquire valuable learning through a variety of experiences ranging from collective decision making to a community garden, and from participatory budgeting to policy development. This learning is often implicit in that many do not know the extent of their own acquisition of skills, knowledge, and dispositions that emanated from their community engagement. We identified three main types of learning: instrumental learning, interpersonal learning, and learning about the role and importance of volunteering. The main conclusion of this study is that organizations seeking to make their community a better place to live are more likely to benefit if their members are engaged in significant learning and have the possibility to reflect individually and collectively on such learning.

From this, three main recommendations arise from our study. First, we propose that if this learning were made explicit more often, community organizations would benefit more from their collective base of knowledge and experience and avoid repeating mistakes. That is, if organizations and individuals are aware of what they already know and have the opportunity to share it with others, they will be able to act that much more wisely in future activities aimed at improving their communities. Moreover, uncovering some of this learning can be the steppingstone for further reflective activity and purposeful action. Second, we suggest that organizations should foster learning by creating appropriate spaces and activities that nurture development of particular skills, knowledge, and attitudes. An example of this is the housing cooperative annual national convention, which brings members from co-ops together and gives them a chance to interact and learn from each other. Third, we recommend that community organizations establish regular mentoring systems by which new volunteers can learn organically from experienced volunteers or from paid workers.

In sum, regular engagement in community organizations produces learning that generates new skills, knowledge, and attitudes that are important for the personal development of volunteers, for the interaction among volunteers, and for the well-being and effectiveness of the organization. Community organizations could benefit significantly from a more intentional approach to learning for volunteers and from a strategy for drawing on what volunteers learn to continue building the organization.

References

Allport, G. W. The Nature of Prejudice. Cambridge, Mass.: Addison-Wesley, 1954.

Belenky, M. F., Bond, L. A., and Weinstock, J. S. A Tradition That Has No Name: Nurturing the Development of People, Families, and Communities. New York: Basic Books, 1997.

Blackstone, A. "'It's Just About Being Fair': Activism and the Politics of Volunteering in the Breast Cancer Movement." Gender and Society, 2004, 18(3), 350–368.

Bloom, L. R., and Kilgore, D. "The Volunteer Citizen After Welfare Reform in the United States: An Ethnographic Study of Volunteerism in Action." Voluntas, 2003, 14(4), 431–454.

Coady, M. M. Masters of Their Own Destiny. New York: Harper and Brothers, 1939.

Colley, H., Hodkinson, P., and Malcom, J. Informality and Formality in Learning. Leeds, UK: Lifelong Learning Institute, 2004.

Dewey, J. Democracy and Education: An Introduction to the Philosophy of Education. New York: Macmillan, 1926 [1916].

Eraut, M. "Non-formal Learning and Tacit Knowledge in Professional Work." *British Journal of Educational Psychology,* 2000, *70*(1), 113–136.

Finger, M. "New Social Movements and Their Implications for Adult Education." *Adult Education Quarterly,* 1989, *40,* 15–22.

Foley, G. *Learning in Social Action: A Contribution to Understanding Informal Education.* New York: Zed, 1999.

Freire, P. *Pedagogy of the Oppressed.* New York: Continuum, 1970.

Hall, B. L. "Participatory Research, Popular Knowledge and Power: A Personal Reflection." *Convergence,* 1981, *14,* 6–19.

Hall, B. L. "Social Movement Learning: Theorizing a Canadian Tradition." In T. Fenwick, T. Nesbit, and B. Spencer (eds.), *Contexts of Adult Education: Canadian Perspectives.* Toronto: Thompson Educational, 2006.

Hall, M., Lasby, D., Gumulka, G., and Tryon, C. *Caring Canadians, Involved Canadians: Highlights from the 2004 Canada Survey of Giving, Volunteering and Participating,* 2006. Retrieved June 1, 2006, from http://www.givingandvolunteering.ca/pdf/CSGVP_Highlights_2004_en.pdf.

Hall, M., McKeown, L. E., and Roberts, K. Caring Canadians, *Involved Canadians: Highlights from the 2000 National Survey of Giving, Volunteering and Participating.* Ottawa: Statistics Canada, 2001.

Handy, F., and others. "Public Perception of 'Who Is a Volunteer': An Examination of the Net-Cost Approach from a Cross-Cultural Perspective." *Voluntas: International Journal of Voluntary and Nonprofit Organizations,* 2000, *11*(1), 45–65.

Kilgore, D. W. "Understanding Learning in Social Movements: A Theory of Collective Learning." *International Journal of Lifelong Education,* 1999, *18,* 191–202.

Lacey, A., and Ilcan, S. "Voluntary Labor, Responsible Citizenship, and International NGOs." *International Journal of Comparative Sociology,* 2006, *47*(1), 34–53.

Lindeman, E. C. *The Meaning of Adult Education.* New York: New Republic, 1926.

Livingstone, D. W., and Scholtz, A. *Work and Lifelong Learning in Canada: Basic Findings of the 2004 WALL Survey,* 2006. Retrieved Mar. 10, 2007, from http://www.wallnetwork.ca/resources/WALLSurveyReportFINALMarch2007.pdf.

Macduff, N. "Societal Changes and the Rise of the Episodic Volunteer." In J. L. Brudney (ed.), *Emerging Areas of Volunteering.* (Arnova Occasional Paper Series.) 2005, *1*(2).

MacPherson, I. *Encouraging Associative Intelligence: Co-operatives, Shared Learning and Responsible Citizenship.* Keynote address at the Conference of the International Association for the Study of Cooperation in Education (IASCE), Manchester, England, June 2002. http://www.iasce.net/publications/manchester_macpherson.shtml.

Mezirow, J., & Associates (eds.). *Learning as Transformation: Critical Perspectives on a Theory in Progress* (1st ed.). San Francisco: Jossey-Bass, 2000.

Miles, A. R. *Integrative Feminisms: Building Global Visions, 1960s-1990s.* New York: Routledge, 1996.

Mitchell, K. "Transnationalism, Neo-liberalism, and the Rise of the Shadow State." *Economy and Society,* 2001, *30*(2), 165–189.

Mündel, K., and Schugurensky, D. "The 'Accidental Learning' of Volunteers: The Case of Community-Based Organizations in Ontario." In K. Künzel (ed.), *International Yearbook of Adult Education.* Cologne: Böhlau-Verlag, 2005.

Polanyi, M. *The Tacit Dimension.* New York: Doubleday, 1966.

Ross-Gordon, J. M., and Dowling, B. "Adult Learning in the Context of African-American Women's Voluntary Organizations." *International Journal of Lifelong Education,* 1995, *14*(4), 306–319.

Salamon, L. M. *America's Nonprofit Sector: A Primer* (2nd ed.). New York: Foundation Center, 1999.

Schugurensky, D. "The Forms of Informal Learning: Towards a Conceptualization of the Field." NALL Working Paper no. 19. Toronto, Ont.: OISE/University of Toronto, 2000.

Schugurensky, D., Mündel, K., and Duguid, F. "Learning from Each Other: Housing Cooperative Members' Acquisition of Skills, Knowledge, Attitudes and Values." *Cooperative Housing Journal*, Fall 2006, 2–15.

KARSTEN MÜNDEL *is the interim director of International, Outdoor and Community Service Learning at the Augustana Campus of the University of Alberta. He teaches and researches in the Global and Development Studies program. He also leads Augustana's exchange in rural Mexico and rural Alberta, which focuses on popular education and community based research.*

DANIEL SCHUGURENSKY *is coordinator of the Adult Education and Community Development Program of the Ontario Institute for Studies in Education of the University of Toronto (OISE/UT). His areas of teaching and research focus on the political economy of education, informal citizenship learning, popular education, participatory democracy, and university-community relationships.*

New Directions for Adult and Continuing Education • DOI: 10.1002/ace

6

Complex choices may confront educators in designing community based learning opportunities for adults; decisions will be influenced by their perspectives on teaching and learning.

Educator as Designer: Balancing Multiple Teaching Perspectives in the Design of Community Based Learning for Adults

Catherine Marienau, Susan C. Reed

Careful course design sets the stage for effective learning, whether in a formal or informal setting. Designers of learning experiences seek a balance among several learning objectives that compete for time in the classroom and for space on the syllabus. The nature of community based learning with adults multiplies the design decisions that must be made in taking into account distinctive characteristics of adult learners. Community based learning programs designed with adult students in mind make accommodations for adults' experiences and skills (Largent and Horinek, Chapter Four of this volume). Those designing reflection activities with volunteers also consider adults' experiences and needs (Mündel and Schugurensky, Chapter Five).

When designing community based learning for adults, educators are also balancing multiple perspectives on teaching, such as their concern with transmission of knowledge along with the developmental value of experiential learning. To make matters even more complex, educators may be

Acknowledgments: The authors thank Anne Rapp for her role in developing these ideas about adults in community based learning. We thank the School for New Learning and the Steans Center for Community Based Service Learning for their support of a symposium, Linking Adults with Community, that helped seed our work on this chapter.

attempting to enhance adult learning while teaching younger and older students in the same classroom. The designer of community based learning is likely to juggle even more objectives than the educator whose course does not include experiential learning, the interests of a community partner, and the need for ongoing reflection. Becoming more aware of multiple and often competing goals can help the designer make difficult choices. Wiggins and McTighe (2005) remind us that "good design is about learning to be thoughtful and specific about our purposes and what they imply"(p. 14). Educators cannot navigate the complex terrain of community based learning with adult students without attending to their own mental models—the assumptions, beliefs, commitments, and roles that a given educator brings to teaching and learning. For example, one educator believes that "if the student hasn't learned, I haven't taught"; another believes that "I teach it, and the student is responsible for learning it." Both are committed to teaching, but they see their roles with regard to learning quite differently.

We begin the chapter by drawing on the adult learning literature for theories and concepts that are fundamental to the design of learning for adults. Experienced educators will recognize that central ideas in adult learning (such as the value of experiential learning, the importance of reflecting on experience, and the social nature of learning) have become essential to the community based learning literature as well. In addition, these principles apply to learning at all ages. They can be used to enhance courses that are entirely populated by adult learners as well as those with a mixture of older and younger students. We then review distinctive characteristics of adult learners that we urge educators to address in their course design. Finally, we consider various perspectives on teaching that educators may draw on in designing their courses. All these aspects of the planning process can be balanced in course design while recognizing the ongoing tensions among them. In this analysis, we call on our own experience with designing community based learning for adults and with focus groups that we conducted with adult students at the School for New Learning at DePaul University during the period of July 2005 through August 2006.

Conceptual Frameworks in Adult Learning

Among the many concepts associated with adult learning and development, we highlight four that are basic to community based learning and particularly relevant to design work. These concepts center on designing for *events* that directly engage learners in dealing with *genuine problems* or situations, while *reflecting* critically on these experiences in *interaction* with others.

Direct Experience. All learning begins with experience (Kolb, 1984), but not all experiences generate learning (Dewey, 1938). This primary principle of learning directs educators to recognize that when the accent is on learning, events can lead to significant meaning making ("making sense of an experience"; Mezirow, 1990, p. 1). Community based learning offers any number of events that could prompt students to test their ideas, based on their experiences, against the realities of people's lives and interpretations of others. As an example, in the context of a community based learning course on homelessness, students often express their initial perception that "homeless people don't work." After spending time interacting with residents in transitional housing, these same students learn that people are homeless for varied and complex reasons and some do, in fact, hold a job.

The importance of context for learning is explained by the theory of situated cognition. A main premise of this theory is that an individual's thinking is influenced significantly by the social context in which her or his experience occurs (Wilson, 1993). Individuals can hold inaccurate perceptions of people who are homeless because their environment has isolated them from the social issue and the real people involved. A rich source for learning would be a community based learning course where the experiences of students' interactions with the residents become one of the texts, along with the subject matter readings and discussion.

Such situations challenge one's ideas and preconceptions. Testing ideas in action (active experimentation) is an element of Kolb's model (1984) of learning effectively from experience. As Zull (2002) explains, "Theory [one's own and others' ideas] must be tested in action in order to complete learning to discover how our understanding matches reality" (p. 7). In Chapter Seven, Fiddler and Marienau offer a model for reflection that helps individuals convert events, such as tutoring in a transitional housing setting, into experiences from which they can derive meaningful learning.

The concept of direct experience invites the designer to organize events that test learners' preconceived ideas. A related concept involves designing situations in which learners are tackling real problems. Coupling direct experience and real situations can engender learning that is particularly meaningful for adults.

Genuine Problems. Keeton, Sheckley, and Griggs (2002) articulate the power of students engaging directly with genuine problems: "A rich body of experience is essential for optimum learning. Those who engage in direct experience of an object of study will normally learn more accurately and penetratingly about it than those who do not experience it directly. . . . Using genuine problems as a focal point of inquiry serves as a catalyst that optimizes the interaction between broadening experience and reflection on it" (p. 6).

Adult students prefer their work in community based activities to be meaningful to the community (Clary and Snyder, 2002), as well as to their own learning. In focus groups with adult students, we heard repeatedly comments such as "I feel I accomplished something meaningful" and "I gained an inner sense of satisfaction that comes from doing something meaningful for others." These students worked with community-initiated projects such as an alternative high school for ex-offenders and a health fair to promote HIV/AIDS awareness among youth.

The students' quotes emphasize the affective domain of learning through doing something "genuine" that benefited others. Illeris (2004) is among many who recognize the important role of emotion in learning. In a given event, it is the nature of the interaction among the three dimensions of learning—cognitive, affective, and social relationship—that shape an individual's learning experience. Potentially powerful situations are those that are dramatically different from students' previous experiences and knowledge, evoking strong emotions and testing assumptions and mental models. As an illustration, a focus group student recalled her initial emotional state before she met with teenage girls at the community agency hosting their group sessions. She anticipated that she would "hear all these stories the first day: 'Mom's on drugs, Dad's on drugs; every little dime I get they take.'" Instead, she heard the girls share intimate feelings about themselves and offer each other a "respectful space" to do that. This student had "walked in angry, thinking 'I'm not coming back. I don't care what you all say.'" But that's not what happened after all. She recalled, "After I left that night, I couldn't wait to get back."

What made her change her mind? Mezirow (2000) might explain that she encountered a disorienting dilemma, prompting her to question currently held assumptions and then shift them to inform future actions (planning to attend the next meeting).

Thus far, an essential element is missing from the story of this student's learning experience. What happened in the space between the event (prompt) and a change in her perceptions (shift)?

Reflection on Experience. The critical element is, of course, reflection, a subtheme in the previous sections. When engaged in thoughtful and reflective learning, "we consider carefully the knowledge, belief, values, skills, etc. with which we have been presented. In these cases we think or reflect carefully and decide whether to accept them or not, and practice them or not" (Jarvis, 2006, p. 29). A focus group student reported grappling with these kinds of tensions. Before she actually had the experience of tutoring men who were formerly incarcerated, her attitude was "you committed the crime, you serve the time. I wasn't all that sympathetic." Through reflecting on her experiences, she noted: "It changed my mind in a lot of ways on how I felt about people that were incarcerated. . . . Being there was very informative. . . . After hearing some of their stories, I really opened up to these people."

In the process of making meaning, this student's prior learning influenced her encounter with a new event. As she illustrates, each individual brings her or his "personal model of reality" (MacKeracher, 2004, p. 34), which presents a structure for approaching new experiences—what gets attention, how meaning is assigned, what skills are involved. Prior learning can be a foundation for new learning, or it can block learning. If the new situation tests someone's model of reality, her brain will search first for something familiar that she can connect with the new situation. If what she draws on from prior learning does not fit, then she ventures into new territory and determines, typically with some struggle or uncertainty, whether and how to engage in the learning process.

To promote learning from experience, reflection is designed to provoke reconsideration of preconceptions and prior experiences. This process is both individual and social.

Social Relationships. As noted in the previous section on direct experience, people learn by observing and interacting with others. The values, behaviors, and images that individuals learn within their primary group influence whether and how they make meaning from experiences outside of the familiar (Kegan, 1994). A principal objective of community based learning has been to introduce students to situations and settings outside their familiar communities as stimulation for questioning—and perhaps adapting, expanding, or changing altogether—their attitudes, beliefs, or behaviors. For adults, because they are mediating prior learning with new situations, changes in these realms can be especially taxing and not easily done alone.

Comparing assumptions, observations, and conclusions, learners expand the opportunities to learn from experience. Relational learning, or connected learning, which has been associated with women's learning (Belenky, Clinchy, Goldberger, and Tarule, 1996; Hayes and Flannery, 2000), seems especially relevant to community based learning. The focus is on holding conversations with others such that an adult learner can "connect with, learn from, or challenge the different experiences and interpretations shared by others" (Fenwick, 2003, p. 58).

Designers of community based learning can foster dialogue that enhances the individual's reflection on experience and helps to solidify interaction between cognitive and emotional responses.

Distinguishing Characteristics of Adult Learners

Educators continue to debate whether adults really differ from younger students in how they learn. We agree with MacKeracher's interpretation (2004) that although "the cognitive and physiological processes involved in learning may indeed be similar for adults and children . . . the social, emotional, developmental, and situational variables that affect learning are different for adults and children" (p. 26). What, then, should an instructor who is designing community based learning know about the distinctions of adults as learners? We are not entering the debate on *how adults learn*. Rather, we highlight six interrelated characteristics of adults (adapted from MacKeracher, 2004) that speak to approaches and strategies that enhance their potential for meaningful learning. Attention to these characteristics enhances the design and overall effectiveness of community based learning offerings.

First, adults constantly negotiate multiple roles and expectations, which center on being productive and responsible to oneself and others.

New Directions for Adult and Continuing Education • DOI: 10.1002/ace

Second, as adults grow older and more mature, their individual differences become more sharply etched. Third, adults seek learning that is relevant to problems, situations, and expectations from real life, rather than discipline-defined subjects. Fourth, adults' new learning involves "transforming or extending the meanings, values, skills, and strategies acquired in previous experience" (MacKeracher, 2004, p. 27). Fifth, adults want to participate in making decisions about their own learning. Sixth, adults' openness to new learning is facilitated through an environment that supports connection and dialogue with others.

Although some of these characteristics are not unique to adults, the richness and complexity of adults' life experiences are qualitatively different from those of younger learners and are rich fodder for learning (Kegan, 1994; Kolb, 1984; Taylor, Marienau, and Fiddler, 2000). The characteristics just noted make adult learners especially good candidates for community based learning. With proper design and facilitation, adults are likely to approach their community based learning assignments with a strong sense of responsibility to themselves and others, sincere interest in the project, openness to new learning, willingness to share their knowledge and skills, and eagerness to share their learning experiences with others.

Perspectives That Influence Design Choices

The perspectives that designers of educational experiences bring to their work influence the choices they make. Educators play multiple roles in the teaching-learning process, and most recognize that each role contributes to an important aspect of students' experience. Achieving a balance among these roles often requires trade-offs, for example between activities that promote development of civic engagement and those that supply important information and ideas.

On the basis of research with hundreds of educators, Pratt (2005) has articulated five perspectives on teaching that constitute a useful framework for grappling with tough choices about key design elements. He calls these perspectives transmission, apprentice, developmental, nurturing, and social reform.

A *transmission* perspective on teaching centers on the educator as deliverer of content. From this vantage point, the "instructional process is shaped and guided by the content" (p. 218).

An *apprentice* perspective positions the educator in modeling ways of being and doing. This represents the notion that "expert knowledge is best learned in contexts of application and practice" (p. 226).

A *developmental* perspective focuses on cultivating higher-order thinking. Here the emphasis is on the "potential emergence of increasingly complex and sophisticated forms of thought related to one's content, discipline, or practice" (p. 234).

A *nurturing* perspective attends foremost to facilitating self-efficacy, "based on a belief in the critical relationship between learners' self-concept and learning" (p. 239). This perspective is centered on qualities of the environment and relationships that are supportive of the individual.

A *social reform* perspective is oriented to seeking a better society. An educator holding this perspective is guided by "an explicit, well articulated . . . ideal and ideology [that] have emerged to a position of dominance and centrality" (p. 246).

Clearly these perspectives are not mutually exclusive. An instructor operates from some combination of perspectives within a given course. Being keenly aware of these perspectives can help instructors make sound design choices with purpose and flexibility.

Key Choices in Designing Community Based Learning with Adults

Important decisions that are made by designers of community based learning courses for adults take into account the distinctive characteristics of adults and the educator's own perspectives on learning and teaching. Here we identify issues that arise for the designer as adults' needs and the educator's goals and objectives are held in creative tension. Tradeoffs are inevitable; in making them more apparent, decisions may be made more confidently.

Flexibility in Accommodating Adults' Busy Lives. Given that adults have multiple responsibilities, one key choice concerns the balance among students' direct experience with the community, coverage of the subject matter, and space for reflection and dialogue. Given that 82 percent of adult students twenty-four and older work, and more than half are married or have dependents (Berker and Horn, 2003; Choy and Premo, 1995), those designing community based learning projects face choices on how to balance reading and other assignments with time spent in the community.

O'Connell (2002) cautions adult educators to make sure that the hours required for a community based project do not exceed those of a traditional course. This may necessitate time for students to collaborate during class or even hold class at the community site. Other accommodations may be needed to allow adults with family responsibilities to participate in community based projects. Darlington-Hope and Jacoby (1999) recommend community placements that allow participation of whole families so that community involvement does not require parents to pay more for day care or leave their family during precious evening or weekend hours. They report that the National Clearinghouse for Commuter Programs looks for agencies as community partners whose projects could include contributions from children and teenagers. At the very least, partnerships should be developed that allow adults to work around their professional schedules, which

New Directions for Adult and Continuing Education • DOI: 10.1002/ace

usually means scheduling work in the community during evenings and weekends.

How far should faculty bend in the number of hours students are required to spend in the community? Practice varies (Jacoby, 1996), but DePaul University (on the quarter schedule) recommends twenty to twenty-five hours as the typical requirement. For many instructors, this may be a tough call. The decision to require fewer hours in the community may reflect the instructor's desire to accommodate adults' demanding schedules or cover more material. Brookfield (2005) advocates that the determining factor should be the instructor's judgment about whether the quantity of time adults spend in and with the community (quality being another factor) will be significant enough to engender critical reflection on their assumptions.

From a transmission perspective, paring coverage of content may be too high a cost. However, combined with a developmental perspective, experiential learning could be a powerful vehicle for students to engage with the reading and stimulate deeper reflection and learning. Smith (Chapter One in this volume) suggests a useful research agenda that would give the education community empirical data on the scope, intensity, and duration of projects that are optimal for adult learning and development.

Reflection on Prior Experience. We know that adults will bring assumptions, emotions, and beliefs developed over time to a new community based learning course. The process by which they reflect on a given event in the community is enhanced by consideration of their previous experiences (Keeton, Sheckley, and Griggs, 2002). This would mean including space for reflection so that adults can identify their past associations with the people, types of organizations, activities, and neighborhoods encountered in their community based learning project. A developmental perspective is prominent in the decision to marry active reflection on past and present experiences. At the same time, expert transmission of knowledge and ideas can also enhance reflection. Taylor, Marienau, and Fiddler's book *Developing Adult Learners: Strategies for Teachers and Trainers* (2000) offers numerous creative strategies for integrating these perspectives.

A related reason to consider incorporating reflection on prior learning is that adults bring knowledge and skills (sometimes at the level of professional expertise) to a community based project. Largent and Horinek (Chapter Four) recommend that community partners, in selecting projects and designing activities, consider the expertise adults bring so that students may contribute what they know and advance their professional learning goals. On the institutional side, for example, Richland College offers co-curricular reflection sessions that help adults identify knowledge gained from involvement with prior community based projects and relate the knowledge to broader theories and concepts (Chickering, Dalton, and Stamm, 2006).

Standards and principles exist that can guide institutions in granting college credit for adults' documentation of their significant learning experiences in social activism, through prior learning assessment (PLA; Fiddler,

Marienau, and Whitaker, 2006). Through PLA, institutions of higher education promote development of adults' ability to reflect on past events and connect their own interpretations to the ideas and theories of others. They can also advocate social reform, as illustrated by efforts in Canada and South Africa to use PLA as a vehicle for economic development (CAEL, 2007).

Attention to Individual Differences. As adults mature, their personal characteristics become increasingly well defined. Facilitators of reflection on community based projects will do well to encourage students to notice and respect individual differences between and among themselves, their classmates, and members of the community. How one perceives others and how one is perceived by others is influenced greatly by the mental models of diverse individuals. Green (2001) relates the experiences of white and African American tutors working with African American kids. Although tutors of color faced initial suspicion from school authorities, they were more successful in the long run in earning the trust of the children and the status of "role model." The experience was an opportunity for white students to reflect on the relevance of race, leading one student to observe, "I am aware of myself for the first time in my life" (Green, 2001, p. 23).

Today's nontraditional students (who Holland and Robinson argue, in Chapter Two, are increasingly traditional) are likely adult; they also are likely to be the first generation to go to college or to be students of color. Community based learning for such students does not necessarily involve the discovery of difficult life conditions, such as poverty. Rather, adult students may be rediscovering or revisiting a community in which they (or their parents) have lived at some point in their lives or still live. Working-class students in higher education may encounter "two selves" while working in the community (Vincent, 2003), identifying as a member of the community because of past experiences but being perceived as an outsider because of their status as a university student (Chesler and Scalera, 2000). At the same time, classroom discussions about "those poor neighborhoods" can leave students for whom that particular community or a similar community is "home" feeling that their experience is being stereotyped, ignored, or demeaned.

Designing a course to make individual differences visible requires the instructor to consciously create a safe place for all students' experiences to be discussed (Brookfield, 2005; Johnson-Bailey, 2002). From a social reform perspective, the instructor encourages students to cross borders of race and class that adults otherwise avoid. But assumptions about others, based on their class, race, sex, and other socially constructed factors may be articulated that are painful for some students to hear. Significant support for those students must be provided, which encourages instructors to tap into their nurturing capacity. Without an intentional and respectful focus on individual differences, some students may struggle to find a forum where they can honestly reflect on their experiences or assumptions, which may be quite different from those of others.

New Directions for Adult and Continuing Education • DOI: 10.1002/ace

Consideration of Adults' Practical Skills and Inclinations. Projects that are designed to help adults accomplish a clearly stated goal within a reasonable time frame engender a sense of accomplishment that adults value. Such projects are particularly effective with adult students because they tap the initiative, project management and other professional skills, and networks that individual adults bring to community based projects. Accustomed to accomplishing multiple tasks every day, adult students especially prefer to end the term having made a tangible contribution to the community's efforts. Community partners, in turn, appreciate the problem-solving skills that adults bring to their collaboration and achievement of a specific product that helps the organization accomplish its mission. Instructors who seek and support this kind of collaboration may be able to integrate developmental, apprentice, and social reform perspectives.

Yet balancing these multiple perspectives can be challenging in the design of a community-based learning course. The service learning and adult learning literatures caution against an apprentice approach that overemphasizes the practical outcomes of learning (Pascuale-Leone and Irwin, 1998; Green, 2001), at the cost of students examining beliefs and assumptions through critical reflection in dialogue with others. Representing a developmental perspective, Mezirow (2000) would advocate having students encounter situations that are dramatically different from their previous experiences, in order to stimulate deeper reflection and new learning.

At the same time, the designer faces a potential trade-off between leading with a social reform perspective or with a combined developmental-nurturing perspective. From the former perspective, the designer will want to allot plenty of time for students to work on a community project, such as a health fair, that makes a clear contribution to the welfare of a community and advances the mission of a partner organization. From a developmental-nurturing orientation, a designer may focus instead on an activity that builds relationships between adults who are different from one another so as to develop students' understanding of diverse cultures. It is quite possible that all these goals can be accomplished in one project. Where a choice must be made, instructors nonetheless can design reflection to enhance adult learning from the complexity of events that occur in the process of community engagement (Taylor, Marienau, and Fiddler, 2000).

Adult Students' Voices in Front-End Decisions. Given adults' inclination to have some say in their own learning, educators must determine how much control to exercise over arranging community based activities. Some faculty encourage students to arrange their own placement with community based organizations to accommodate and build on networks that adults have already established in their communities. Kirlin (2002) argues that this "front end" of a community based learning course offers students the opportunity to develop and practice such civic engagement skills as assessing community problems, identifying who is working to address them, and determining what role they can productively play in this work.

New Directions for Adult and Continuing Education • DOI: 10.1002/ace

Yet many community based learning courses are designed with the assistance of centers that arrange placement for students, negotiate activities in advance, and maintain relationships with community partners. This arrangement offers some stability for the community partner and streamlines the placement process when the university routinely places waves of students. Prearranged placements also allow students to spend more time in the community, without weeks of the term being lost to front-end communication with community sites. On the other hand, from a nurturing perspective educators may decide to emphasize development of students' self-efficacy over the benefits of more time spent in the community.

The choice to involve adults in planning a community based activity requires the instructor to engage the student in active reflection on learning goals and assumptions. When anticipating community based projects, students will want to consider the level of expertise they bring to the work, not simply to arrange appropriate activities but to ensure they will be prompted to identify and question their assumptions. Adults with a broad background in corporate marketing, for instance, may assume that this expertise prepares them to assist in promoting a not-for-profit organization (Reed and Rapp, 2000). Even though the competencies that adults bring to the project are relevant, their skills may not be transferred as readily as expected. Students will want to surface their assumptions, consider areas in which they are a novice, and employ skills of observation and question asking before diving in.

Building Relationships.   Considering the importance of connection and dialogue to adult learning, the designer of a community based learning course chooses how much to emphasize intentional development of relationships within the class and within the community. Most instructors have witnessed the significant learning that occurs in a classroom for students who are openly and honestly reflecting on events that occur in the community. As trust between these individuals grows, students ask questions, compare responses, and grow from analysis of others' interpretations (Fiddler and Marienau, Chapter Seven).

Development of trust can be a course objective that a facilitator intentionally attends to; or it may happen (or not) depending on serendipity or the interpersonal skills of the adults in the group. As mentioned earlier, instructors who seek to foster relationships between individuals in a diverse cluster of students must help them pay careful attention to both shared and divergent experiences.

Relationships that develop in an organization among adult students, staff, and community residents can be similarly rich in learning opportunities for all parties, if approached with an assumption of equality (an important value to foster from a social reform perspective). Students often report the significant learning that results from even the simplest interaction with someone they assumed was different. Surfacing such preconceptions enhances learning, and it could help ensure that community residents do not suffer condescension or even hostility in their exchange with students.

New Directions for Adult and Continuing Education • DOI: 10.1002/ace

Instructors who wish to foster learning from such interactions draw on their nurturing perspective to promote elements of healthy relationships (Bringle and Hatcher, 2002) and encourage students to seek out an organization's staff, who likely will appreciate the educational purpose of communication on site. Students often report the value of their contact with staff and regret when opportunities for interaction are few (Largent and Horinek, Chapter Four). Building true relationships takes time. But community based learning courses that encourage developing relationships in the community may improve the likelihood of adult students continuing their work in the community once the term ends, and over time. Educators who can influence this kind of outcome illustrate a rich blending of various perspectives on teaching (Pratt, 2005).

Conclusion

A rich literature on adult learning guides the educator in designing opportunities for experiential, project-based learning as well as reflection with others that compares prior experiences. In addition, considering the distinctive characteristics of adult learners, efforts are made to accommodate adults' multiple roles, as well as their interest in practical outcomes and self-directedness. In making these choices, designers attempt to balance such concerns as development of adult learners' understanding of themselves and others with promotion of significant change in partnership with community organizations.

Prescriptions and formulas for designing community based learning do not exist; if they did, we would be wary of them. Each community based learning course has its own complexion, shaded by the numerous factors we have discussed. Our main point is that all of these factors should be addressed purposely to help make the learning experience as optimal as possible for each adult student and for the group as a whole. As every experienced teacher knows, all the careful design up front still does not guarantee a success. Design is an iterative process, which involves planning before the course begins, making adjustments during the course, and revising for the next offering. Our intent is that the frameworks and perspectives presented in this chapter will inspire and inform educators of adults in community based settings.

References

Belenky, M. F., Clinchy, B. M., Goldberger, N. R., and Tarule, J. M. *Women's Ways of Knowing: Development of Self, Voice and Mind* (2nd ed.). New York: Basic Books, 1996. (First published 1986)

Berker, A., and Horn, L. "Work First, Study Second: Adult Undergraduates Who Combine Employment and Post Secondary Enrollment." *U.S. Department of Education, National Center for Education Statistics.* NCES 2003–267, Washington, D.C., 2003.

Bringle, R. G., and Hatcher, J. A. "Campus-Community Partnerships: The Terms of Engagement." *Journal of Social Issues,* 2002, *58*(3), 503–516.

Brookfield, S. *Developing Critically Reflective Teachers.* San Francisco: Jossey-Bass, 2005.

CAEL. *Prior Learning Assessment at Home and Abroad: Excerpts from Recent Articles in the CAEL Forum and News.* Chicago: CAEL, 2007.

Chesler, M., and Scalera, C. V. "Race and Gender Issues Related to Service Learning Research." *Michigan Journal of Community Service Learning,* 2000, *Special Issue,* Fall, 18–27.

Chickering, A. W., Dalton, J. C., and Stamm, L. *Encouraging Authenticity and Spirituality in Higher Education.* San Francisco: Jossey-Bass, 2006.

Choy, S., and Premo, M. D. "Profile of Older Undergraduates, 1989–1990." *U.S. Department of Education, National Center for Education Statistics,* 1995.

Clary, E. G., and Snyder, M. "Community Involvement: Opportunities and Challenges in Socializing Adults to Participate in Society." *Journal of Social Issues,* 2002, *58*(3), 581–591.

Darlington-Hope, M., and Jacoby, B. "Service Learning and the Nontraditional Student." *Compact Current,* 1999, *13*(3), 1–5.

Dewey, J. *Experience and Education.* New York: Collier, 1938.

Eyler, J., and Giles, D. *Where's the Learning in Service-Learning?* San Francisco: Jossey-Bass, 1999.

Fenwick, T. J. *Learning Through Experience: Troubling Orthodoxies and Intersecting Questions.* Malabar, Fla.: Krieger, 2003

Fiddler, M., Marienau, C., and Whitaker, U. *Assessing Learning: Standards, Principles, and Procedures.* Dubuque, Iowa: Kendall/Hunt, 2006.

Green, A. E. "'But You Aren't White': Racial Perceptions and Service Learning." *Michigan Journal of Community Service Learning,* Fall 2001, 18–26.

Hayes, E., and Flannery, D. *Women as Learners: The Significance of Gender in Adult Learning.* San Francisco: Jossey-Bass, 2000.

Illeris, K. *Adult Education and Adult Learning.* Malabar, Fla.: Krieger, 2004.

Jacoby, B., and Associates. *Service Learning in Higher Education Concepts and Practices.* San Francisco: Jossey-Bass, 1996.

Jarvis, P. *Towards a Comprehensive Theory of Human Learning.* New York: Routledge, 2006.

Johnson-Bailey, J. "Race Matters: The Unspoken Variable in the Teaching-Learning Transaction." In J. Ross-Gordon (ed.), *Contemporary Viewpoints on Teaching Adults Effectively.* New Directions in Adult and Continuing Education, no. 93. San Francisco: Jossey-Bass, 2002.

Keeton, M., Sheckley, B., and Griggs, J. *Effectiveness and Efficiency in Higher Education for Adults: A Guide for Fostering Learning.* Dubuque, Iowa: Kendall/Hunt, 2002.

Kegan, R. *In Over Our Heads: The Mental Demands of Modern Life.* Cambridge, Mass.: Harvard University Press, 1994.

Kirlin, M. "Civic Skill Building: The Missing Component in Service Programs?" *PS: Political Science and Politics,* 2002, *35*(3), 571–575.

Kolb, D. *Experiential Learning: Experience as the Source of Learning and Development.* Upper Saddle River, N.J.: Prentice Hall, 1984.

MacKeracher, D. *Making Sense of Adult Learning.* Toronto: University of Toronto Press, 2004.

Mezirow, J. *Fostering Critical Reflection in Adulthood.* San Francisco: Jossey-Bass, 1990.

Mezirow, J. *Learning as Transformation.* San Francisco: Jossey-Bass, 2000.

O'Connell, T. "A Matter of Experience: Service-Learning and the Adult Student." In E. Zlotkowski (ed.), *Service-Learning and the First-Year Experience: Preparing Students for Personal Success and Civic Responsibility.* (Monograph no. 34, pp. 39–50). Columbia: National Resource Center for the First-Year Experience and Students in Transition, University of South Carolina, 2002.

Pascuale-Leone, J., and Irwin, R. R. "Abstraction, the Will, the Self, and the Modes of Learning in Adulthood." In C. Smith and T. Pourchot (eds.), *Adult Learning and Development: Perspectives from Educational Psychology*. London: Erlbaum, 1998.

Pratt, D., and Associates. *Five Perspectives on Teaching in Adult and Higher Education*. Malabar, Fla.: Krieger, 2005.

Reed, S. C., and Rapp, A. "Developing Service Learning Methodologies for Adults." Presented to the Midwest Campus Compact Annual Conference, Chicago, Oct. 2000.

Taylor, K., Marienau, C., and Fiddler, M. *Developing Adult Learners: Strategies for Teachers and Trainers*. San Francisco: Jossey-Bass, 2000.

Vincent, C. (ed.) *Social Justice, Education and Identity*. London: Routledge Palmer, 2003.

Wiggins, G., and McTighe, J. *Understanding by Design*. (2nd ed.) Upper Saddle River, N.J.: Pearson Prentice Hall, 2005.

Wilson, A. L. "The Promise of Situated Cognition." In S. B. Merriam (ed.), *An Update on Adult Learning*. New Directions for Adult and Continuing Education, no. 57. San Francisco: Jossey-Bass, 1993.

Zull, J. *The Art of Changing the Brain*. Sterling, Va.: Stylus, 2002.

CATHERINE MARIENAU *is professor and faculty mentor in the School for New Learning, DePaul University.*

SUSAN C. REED *is associate professor and faculty mentor in the School for New Learning, DePaul University.*

7

Students' formation of meaningful learning through community based activities varies with the nature and quality of reflective skills they develop and apply.

Developing Habits of Reflection for Meaningful Learning

Morris Fiddler, Catherine Marienau

Adoption of community based learning by institutions of higher education comes at a time when, as Chickering declares in the next chapter, our society "cries for more intelligence and more soul in our democracy." Now is an opportune time to engage all students, younger and older, in working toward the social and civic stabilization necessary for a thriving society. An equally compelling prospect is for students to actively immerse themselves in experiences from which they may practice and expand their capacity for creating meaningful learning.

Community based learning and education can be viewed from at least two perspectives. One is a lens that focuses on engagement with service to the community, with all of the explicit and implicit values reflected by those contexts and activities. Another focuses on the learning and associated processes, objects for consideration in and of themselves. The essence of engaging in community based learning is the imperative to *learn from* the service and community experience(s) rather than to *learn about* them. Further understanding about and continuous improvement of community based learning may lie at the intersection of the context and the process.

Many of the authors in this volume point to the importance of reflection as a requisite mediator between the experiences of students and the meaning they make of those experiences—the interweaving of thinking, doing, and feeling (Schön, 1983; Boud, Keogh, and Walker, 1985; Rogers, 2001). We concur. We believe also that the quality of reflection is a measure of higher-order learning and may be a precursor to its development as well

WILEY
InterScience®
DISCOVER SOMETHING GREAT

New Directions for Adult and Continuing Education, no. 118, Summer 2008 © 2008 Wiley Periodicals, Inc.
Published online in Wiley InterScience (www.interscience.wiley.com) • DOI: 10.1002/ace.297

(Smith, Chapter One; Chickering, Chapter Eight). We also assert, on the basis of our own years of experience working with adult students and our reading of the literature, that for many adult students reflection does not happen easily on command. Similar to directives such as "establish rapport" and "be creative," the capability to "reflect on the meaning of your experience" requires both an understanding of the concept and the skills to actually apply it.

Our intentions in this chapter are several: to concentrate on the learning dimension of community based learning; to elevate the role of reflection as an essential bridge between experience and learning; to examine the nature and requisite skills of reflection; and to offer a practical model that can be used to help students (and teachers) practice, develop, and refine their competence in reflection and meaning making. In our model, reflection is required to convert an event—something that someone participates in or that happens during a community based learning project—to an experience from which learning and meaning can emerge. We then discuss some implications of the model for making key decisions in designing and facilitating community based learning projects and programs. Finally, we note some of the risks involved in encouraging a citizenry skilled in reflective learning and practice.

Reflection as Inquiry

Reflection is inquiry into one's experience. It leads with the intent of converting experience(s) into meaningful learning and "to enable better choices or actions in the future as well as enhance one's overall effectiveness" (Rogers, 2001, p. 41). As such, reflection requires active participation in the events of our lives, accompanied by a persistent inner or external voice asking, "What's getting my attention?" The intent of using this simple question as the starting point for an internal inquiry process is to help the learner develop sensitivities to stimuli, and over time to grow the capacity for attending to the details and the nuances of our lives (Hanh, 1999; Langer, 1997; Gelb, 1998; Shapiro, Carlson, Astin, and Freedman, 2006). This starting point is based on the premise that heightened awareness of what we see, hear, touch, feel, think, taste, and smell—especially accompanied by a nonjudging attitude of appreciation—generates greater possibilities to answer the "attention getting" question. Consequently, possibilities are expanded for what may be learned in and from any particular event.

Forms of Attention

Koch (2004) identifies three forms of attention. *Ambient* concerns the attention we give and then minimize to the white noise around us; whatever the stimuli, it quickly fades into the background. *Focal* is the attention we give because someone else, perhaps a teacher, directs us to put our attention on something in particular. *Salient* is the attention given to what stands out to me though not necessarily to you. It is the latter that is most likely to lead to the most meaningful learning. In a service learning project, the teacher may point a student toward paying attention to what the teacher or the curriculum deems to be important or necessary (for example, the National Association of Social Workers' Code of Ethics, as suggested by Richter-Hauk and Arias in Chapter Three); however, that point may or may not be salient to any particular student. Saliency tends to lead to questions such as "What are *my* observations—what am I seeing?" "What might interest me? What am *I* curious about?" "What feelings are evoked; how do I feel about what has gotten my attention?" (In other words, what are the emotional hues that accompany what is being noticed?) These and similar questions help us characterize or name an experience and its attention-getting elements. For example, a female adult student who is tutoring male ex-offenders may notice, and be surprised by, the "protectiveness of these men toward me"; another female student, in the same setting, focuses on "feeling nervous about going in the room with those men."

One of the attributes of reflection is that the inquiry seems most often triggered by an unusual—a salient—event or situation, often though not necessarily a perplexing one (Mezirow, 2000). For example, an adult student recounted what she noticed on arriving for the first time at a chat session among teenage girls: "It's 6:00 P.M. and I am the only white person there. I am older than the girls by many years." As soon as she entered the room, "it became dead silent. . . . I thought, 'I've ruined the mood . . . and I can't be productive.' So I sat in a chair against the wall. . . ." She was fascinated by what seemed to her like a lot of chatter and moving around. "But when it came down to it, it was a very structured environment; they had an agenda . . . they were very honest with each other, which I thought was a really refreshing thing" (from Marienau and Reed's study for Chapter Six).

Event to Experience. We have drawn here a distinction between an event—something has occurred but the aspects are undifferentiated—and the experience of that event, where salient aspects are more sharply distinguished for a given individual. The distinction between event and experience is perhaps best illustrated by the simple observation that two or more individuals participating in the same community based learning activity are very unlikely to pay attention to the same things and have the same experience. This is especially the case if each person is given the encouragement and room to practice differentiating between what is salient for that person and expected (focalized attention) by someone else. For example, two adult students revealed how they felt about being based in a half way house for male ex-offenders. One student, who had had a negative volunteer experience previously, was "afraid" of being "put with a certain element." The other student, who had grown up in that community and moved away at age twenty, said things "felt familiar," and she was comfortable being with "the same guys that I grew up with" (from Marienau and Reed's study for Chapter Six).

New Directions for Adult and Continuing Education • DOI: 10.1002/ace

What is salient and what is "focalized" may be one and the same, but often they are not. The distinctions between an event and an experience, and between what is salient and what is expected, become increasingly important as the question turns to what meaning individuals derive from their experience.

Meaningful Learning and Meaning Making

In the context of higher-level learning, a more complex question should be posed: What meaning do individuals make as they interpret their own experience in light of others' interpretations, and vice versa? Allowing one's own ideas, theories, and beliefs to be informed by the ideas, theories, and beliefs of others in order to interpret one's experience(s) characterizes rich reflection. Why would one ignore or not seek out (and sharpen skills of finding out) what others have expressed in various venues about similar things that got their attention? Whereas each person's experience may be unique to the individual, reliance on just one's own ideas and interpretations is likely to limit meaning-making potential. Conversely, why would one rely only on others' ideas at the risk of losing or not even developing one's own voice and insights?

Meaningful learning involves questioning and examining one's assumptions, beliefs, mental models, values, and a host of other qualities that characterize meaning. It involves asking "What do I believe about this?" "What are other possibilities, other ways of seeing or believing?" "What have others examined and expressed about this?" The quality of reflection, in this schema, rests on forming habits and skills to seek out multiple data points, multiple perspectives, and particularly evidence contrary to one's assumptions and beliefs. The challenge is to hold confirming and disconfirming interpretations simultaneously and, without rushing to judgment in the midst of the endeavor, weave them into one's own take on things.

Where does this all lead? In the best-case scenario, an inquiry into one's experiences (reflection) results in forming and integrating a new understanding of one's experiences that can inform future experiences (Dewey, 1938; Mezirow, 2000; Rogers, 2001), and perhaps a new or revised understanding that can benefit others.

Elements of Meaning Making. Significance is a quality of meaning making that only the individual can assign to the outcome of reflection. The weight of what is significant, and perhaps the degree of confidence to express it publicly, is influenced by the nature and quality of one's path of inquiry. Only the individual can generate her or his responses to these starting and concluding questions: "What got my attention?" "What is its meaning to me?" Meaning, however, is not characterized just by personal significance. Other key elements include connections made to what one already knew or believed, movement from understanding to action, new beliefs, awareness of emotional nuances, and persistent development of skills.

New Directions for Adult and Continuing Education • DOI: 10.1002/ace

**Table 7.1. Elements of Reflection and Reflective Practice(s):
Inquiring into Experience**

Elements of Inquiry	Aspects of Reflection
Requires active participation	With attention to "What's getting my attention?" With an expanding repertoire of "attention" skills and sensitivities
Often initiated or triggered by unusual or perplexing event or situation	Focused by: • What was salient in the event? • What might interest me? • What am I curious about? • What emotions or feelings am I aware of?
Involves examining and interpreting one's beliefs, responses, assumptions, and habits in light of the situation at hand	Most expansive when considering multiple possibilities; actively seeking disconfirming evidence for one's beliefs and assumptions; drawing on the ideas and voices of self and others Places theories and ideas—one's own and others'—in the position of being interpreters and explainers of experiences and observations
Results in integration of a new understanding of one's experiences	Increases the likelihood of learning from the "next event" Expands the possibilities for what one may notice "the next time" Leads to decisions for action with increased conviction Converts information to knowledge and connects the "old" to the "new"

All of these elements are brought to the next event and influence what gets one's attention the next time. These are some of the characteristics of meaningful learning, which is the ultimate intention of reflective inquiry. All of these dimensions of learning increase the likelihood of further learning, of altering and expanding sensitivity to what may be attention-getting, of answering "What might I do differently?" and of deepening the conviction behind an answer to "What might I do that is of value?" Mündel and Schugerensky (Chapter Five) arrived at similar conclusions *cum* recommendations when they listened to and studied actively engaged community volunteers. Table 7.1 summarizes the four elements of reflection just described.

When to Engage in Reflection. The simple answer to the question of *when* is "any time, all the time." In the design process for a course, however, the frequency and timing of invitations or expectations to engage in a reflective process are most likely to be governed by the extent to which advancement of reflective capacity and skills is an intended or explicit outcome of the curriculum. In a given course, building students' reflective capacity may be approached in different ways. On one end of the spectrum, the focus is students' reflections on their experiences in the community; on the other end, reflection is one of a variety of strategies to digest and gain mastery over the field-based content. This poses a decision point for an instructor that would obviously inform the *when* and *to what extent* questions concerning reflection. Like any other question to which an answer falls along a continuum, clear decisions are found only near the extremes. Arriving at a decision somewhere between the extremes, for practical purposes of designing and implementing a class or program, primarily relies on reiterative assessment of student outcomes measured against the intentions of a teacher or the agreements of whoever is governing the curriculum.

A before-during-after framework is an easy starting point to build from (Eyler, 2001). One of the defining characteristics of adults compared to younger students is accumulated experience. Thus it makes good sense to draw on one of the goals of reflective practices to help elevate assumptions, beliefs, and current awareness. It is also fruitful to mine adult students' prior state of knowledge regarding community and service engagements that they are bringing to a project prior to its initiation (Largent and Horinek, Chapter Four). Leading with reflection as a before activity involves asking what has gotten an individual's attention over the course of life as to community, issues to be addressed, the people she or he will work with, and other relevant aspects of the course. Addressing an adult student's prior experience can help make more visible her or his knowledge and beliefs, as well as sense of self and other. Darlington-Hope (2005) illustrated the power of applying this approach as she reflected on the distinctions between citizenship and social service skills, the power relationships embedded in the language of service, the impact of deriving community contribution from self-interest(s), and the implications of participating in a democratic culture. Reflective activities done as a group and with the anticipated community partners expand the scope of this benchmarking activity, which is easily returned to at a later date with the guiding question of "What's changed?"

Building expectations for reflection into a community based learning project is a common practice. What may be less common is allowing the time and space for practice and critical feedback on each person's reflective activities and skill building. Almost anything that has been suggested by authors as a useful reflective technique—structured journals, discussions, blogging, debriefings of lessons learned, readings to connect, and providing contextual perspectives on community based activities—can be useful as a vehicle for students to engage in reflection as a bridge from what they are doing to what they may (should?) be learning. By making room to practice each of the elements of reflection (Table 7.1), with feedback as a gauge for assessing the quality of how those elements are being addressed, it is more likely that reflective capabilities will be treated as skills and improved.

There are certainly some useful rubrics for helping a student form reflective habits of mind. Most of them focus on consolidating and explaining

New Directions for Adult and Continuing Education • DOI: 10.1002/ace

what a student has learned and less on the progressive practice of sensitivities to expand awareness and attention. A nice example of a rubric has been
published under the name of articulated learning (Ash and Clayton, 2004),
which moves from "What did I learn?" through "How, specifically, did I learn
it?" to "Why does this learning matter?" and on to "In what ways will I use
this learning?" At every step, a formal connection to the concepts and issues
of the community based learning objectives is built into this scaffolding to
promote a critical interplay between the focalized attention students are
asked to give in the course of their class activities and the larger, more gen-
eralizable ideas designated by the instructor as most important. Similarly,
with an emphasis on developing awareness and adherence to professional
standards, Richter-Hauk and Arias (Chapter Three) furnished social work
students with a space to find the interpretive nexus among the field activities, the course readings, and their analyses. We would also point to their
example of two boys recognizing a cousin-in-common as a moment to question the assumption of the role culture plays in compassion to other. An
alternative explanation might concern the dynamics derived from evolu-
tionary psychology, hypothesizing that such instances illustrate natural selection for kinship affiliations and altruism.

   All courses come to an end, and reflection on a private and public basis is
a common way to mark students' formal participation in the community and
service activities. Individual essays; cooperative and collaborative production
of murals, presentations, or other expressions of meaningful learning; and dia-
logues with or presentations to the community partners are all avenues for
closing reflective ceremonies. At each point along the beginning–middle–end
timeframe, we advocate thoughtful consideration as to where the accent is
going to be: on what was learned, on how whatever got a student's attention
is being processed through a disciplined reflective process, or on the product
that will be taken as evidence of learning. The message to students regarding
the institutional or faculty regard and valuing of reflective practices is likely to
be conveyed at these junctions.

Learning from Experience: The Reason for Reflection

Reflection is not an activity isolated from a larger dynamic of learning.
Indeed, it is probably just one of a number of processes that we will eventually come to understand as to how learning transpires and meaning is
made or discovered. We have been describing reflection without referenc-
ing this point explicitly, but in order to carry this piece further we will make
the mental model behind our comments visible. There is no shortage of useful models and visualizations of process by which we can both describe learning from experience and derive some implications for practice as teachers.
Here is another that consolidates what we have been describing.

   To lead into this model, we briefly step back to note that the distinction
between experiential learning and learning from experience is frequently

glossed over in the literature on learning (Fiddler, Marienau, and Whitaker, 2006). Though the two phrases—experiential learning and learning from experience—are often used interchangeably, they are not the same. The distinction between the inputs and the outcomes of learning is a useful entrée into the difference between these two expressions. Experiential learning is best associated with the nature of learning activities themselves in which the learner is directly in touch with the realities being studied (Keeton and Tate, 1978). In contrast, learning from experience is the outcome of processes (in other words, what meaning something holds) that accompany experiential learning. Sheckley and Keeton (1999) connected two of their six principles of adult learning to help bring experiential learning and learning from experience together: a rich body of experience is essential for learning to occur best, and experience yields explicit knowledge only if reflected on.

With those distinctions made, we reference four concepts that we have been drawing on in this chapter—events, experiences, reflection, and meaningful learning—and visualize their relationships, as seen in Figure 7.1.

Figure 7.1. Events Model of Learning from Experience

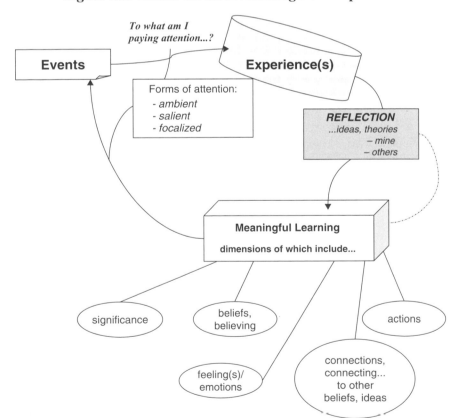

This model distinguishes first between an event in one's life and one's experience of it. Participation in an event spans a spectrum from passive to active, as well as another spectrum, from immersion to degrees of simple absorption. Participation, engagement, involvement, detachment, indifference: the language to describe what transpires for anyone in an event is extensive yet not wholly adequate to describe it, in part because what transpires is subject to individual differences. We have attempted to capture this phenomenon through the simple question referenced several times: "What's got my attention?" The answer to this question, to the extent that it can ever be fully or satisfyingly answered, distinguishes an event from the experience of it. Conversion, then, of an experience to meaningful learning is the role of reflection. What a student puts her or his attention toward—the object of reflection, and how she or he does that, the process of reflection—is the heart of learning from experience.

The implications of this model for both understanding learning from experience and for designing educational events such as community based learning projects or courses are many. We next highlight some of them (and certainly assume that there are others).

The Role of Others' Ideas. The role of theory or interpretive ideas from authors, experts, individual insights, and colleagues becomes situated in a different place than is often the case in common teaching practices. The common practice of leading a class or assignment with selected readings may serve very well to orient a relative novice to a new situation; it also serves to focus one's attention and limit what actually may be salient to someone. This model, however, situates theories following identification of what has gotten one's attention—the experience—rather than preceding it. Useful and valid theories or significant ideas from respected specialists originate from interpretive insights into experiences and observations; indeed, it is how they become known as such. Theories, models, and ideas can play the same role in someone else's experience—the reflective interpretation of both one's and others' experiences and observations. Thus, if reflective practice is an intended outcome of a course or project, the challenge of identifying what is salient to each person accompanied by the support of who and what are possible sources of explanation and how to find them—as well as practiced effort at generating interpretations from individuals' existing frames of reference and knowledge—becomes the sequence by design and supplants "common teaching practices."

Repertoire of Competencies. Sensitivity to what gets one's attention rests on the capacity of one's senses, conceptual frameworks, mental models, facility with perceptual complexities, preferences, and a host of other qualities best described as a repertoire of competencies. The arrows sweeping back from *meaningful learning* to *events* (the attention-based mediator to experiences), and to *reflection* (see Figure 7.1) are meant to illustrate how such a repertoire is developed and functions. The content of the repertoire will assuredly vary from person to person, but in simple terms it can never be too large. Development, use, and retention of this repertoire for both creating and interpreting experiences are, in our estimation, not only a worthy goal of education but a primary one. The experiential basis of community based learning is an excellent context for this.

Tensions Between Individual and Institution. Let us assume there is value in developing an individual's sensitivities to recognizing what is salient to him or her and then apply intelligent reflective analysis to it. Inherent in this assumption is the likely collision between the responsibility of education and what is or might be salient to the individual, or even a group of students on their way to arriving at what is meaningful learning. As an institution, education structures and directs students' attention to what a teacher believes or is charged with transmitting as important to pay attention to (focal attention).

It is common among community based learning instructors to envision outcomes that they want to see with respect to students' values and behavior. What is an instructor to do when those values and behaviors do not emerge, or when students return from their community events with stereotypes that have been reinforced (such as, "The homeless are lazy and just need to work as hard as I do to overcome their hardships")? The temptation may be great to lecture about the systemic causes for laziness, to ensure that the outcome of the event has not simply ended in perpetuation of such stereotypes. This is certainly understandable; instructors' value commitments often run deep, and they have exerted considerable effort to offer rich community based learning experiences.

No one wants to foster harmful stereotypes and uncritical thinking. An ironic reversal could be that through encountering conditions of societal divisions and hegemony, some students come to see the institution of education through this lens. An important decision point that can distinguish educational goals from meaningful learning is the extent to which the nature of a course and instruction foster the space and guidance for students to follow the trail of their reflections to multiple, unpopular, or unintended interpretations of the contextual influences on their community experiences.

Conclusion

The growth of reflective capacities and skills is probably cyclical and progressive, involving affective and cognitive processes (Green, 2007; Damasio, 2003) that may be separable only for analytic purposes. Intentional development of these capacities is, similarly, likely to mediate an adult's continued facility to integrate the complexities that Kolb (1984) profiles as development itself. The capacity to hold and stay aware of what is deemed to be important as a member of a society and to thoughtfully and critically (re)interpret those understandings, and challenge them, is a quality of a soulful, intelligent, and thoughtful society for which we may indeed be crying out (Chickering, Chapter Eight)—and which may also carry unpredictable implications in itself, should a citizenry develop the reflective capabilities and capacities represented here.

References

Ash, S. L., and Clayton, P. H. "The Articulated Learning: An Approach to Guided Reflection and Assessment." *Innovative Higher Education,* 2004, *29,* 137–154.

Boud, D., Keogh, R., and Walker, D. *Turning Reflection into Learning.* New York: Routledge-Farmer, 1985.

Damasio, A. *Looking for Spinoza: Joy, Sorrow, and the Feeling Brain.* Orlando: Harcourt, Brace, 2003.

Darlington-Hope, M. "Keynote Address." Symposium on Linking Adults with Community, DePaul University, Chicago, Oct. 2005.

Dewey, J. *Experience and Education.* New York: Collier, 1963. (Originally published 1938.)

Eyler, J. "Creating Your Reflection Map." In M. Canada and B. W. Speck (eds.), *Developing and Implementing Service-Learning Programs.* New Directions for Higher Education, no. 114. San Francisco: Jossey-Bass, 2001.

Fiddler, M., Marienau, C., and Whitaker, U. *Assessing Learning: Standards, Principles, and Procedures.* Dubuque, Iowa: Kendall/Hunt, 2006.

Gelb, M. *How to Think Like Leonardo da Vinci: Seven Steps to Genius Every Day.* New York: Dell, 1998.

Green, P. M. "Parallel Processes of Transformation: How Student Reflection in Service-Learning Mirrors Faculty Teaching and Learning." Paper presented at the 7th International Research Conference on Service-Learning and Community Engagement, Loyola University Chicago, Oct. 6–9, 2007.

Hanh, T. N. *The Miracle of Mindfulness.* Boston: Beacon Press, 1999.

Keeton, M. T., and Tate, P. J. (eds.) *Learning by Experience: What, Why, How.* New Directions for Experiential Learning, no. 1. San Francisco: Jossey-Bass, 1978.

Koch, C. *The Quest for Consciousness: A Neurobiological Approach.* Englewood, Colo.: Roberts, 2004.

Kolb, D. *Experiential Learning: Experience as the Source of Learning and Development.* Upper Saddle River, N.J.: Prentice Hall, 1984.

Langer, E. *The Power of Mindful Learning.* Reading, Mass.: Addison-Wesley, 1997.

Mezirow, J., and Associates. *Learning As Transformation: Critical Perspectives on a Theory in Progress.* San Francisco: Jossey-Bass, 2000.

Rogers, R. "Reflection in Higher Education: A Concept Analysis." *Innovative Higher Education,* 2001, *26,* 37–57.

Schön, D. *The Reflective Practitioner: How Professionals Think in Action.* New York: Basic Books, 1983.

Shapiro, S. L., Carlson, L. E., Astin, J. A., and Freedman, B. "Mechanisms of Mindfulness." *Journal of Clinical Psychiatry,* 2006, *62,* 373–386.

Sheckley, B., and Keeton, M. *Perspectives on Key Principles of Adult Learning.* Chicago: CAEL, 1999.

MORRIS FIDDLER and CATHERINE MARIENAU are professors and faculty mentors in the School for New Learning, DePaul University.

8

Community based learning among adults is needed to help fuel civic engagement to rebuild and sustain our nation's democracy.

Strengthening Democracy and Personal Development through Community Engagement

Arthur W. Chickering

Reflecting on the experiences, ideas, and commitments represented in this volume brings to mind something I wrote more than twenty years ago:

> Frenzied, unbridled passion, whether in love or work, seldom serves us well. Indeed, it often harms more than helps. To be enflamed, carried away, by an affection, ideology, or cause is easy but such a state shrinks from reflective thought, public scrutiny, and tough minded testing. Maintaining a steady fire that is critical as well as creative is more difficult, especially when it suffers frequent doses of icy logic and frigid resistance. Cool passion seeks fulfillment by joining forces of heart and mind, commitment and critical analysis [1981, p. 783].

This posture is needed more than ever in a society that cries for more intelligence and more soul in our democracy, where we are fed sound bites and misinformation. We need the kind of civic engagement that is advocated in this volume on adults in community based learning.

These next few pages urge us toward practical actions that can augment key dimensions of personal development necessary for effective citizenship. Included are behaviors that strengthen our democracy, such as portrayed by Bill Moyers (2001): "The soul of democracy—the essence of the word itself—is government of, by, and for the people. And the soul of democracy

NEW DIRECTIONS FOR ADULT AND CONTINUING EDUCATION, no. 118, Summer 2008 © 2008 Wiley Periodicals, Inc.
Published online in Wiley InterScience (www.interscience.wiley.com) • DOI: 10.1002/ace.298

is dying. . . . Democracy won't survive if citizens turn into lemmings. . . . The greatest sedition would be our silence" (p. 12).

Consider the challenges facing our federal, state, and local politicians, policy makers, and diverse vested interests. We need to strengthen and sustain a multicultural, multiethnic, multireligious, internationally interdependent, pluralistic democracy. We need to identify and support policies, practices, and resource allocations that anticipate the dislocations and disruptions that will accompany global warming and the steady depletion of oil reserves. We need to contain and help ameliorate recurrent intertribal, interethnic, and interreligious conflicts. We need to address basic issues concerning public education, health care, and an aging population. We need to create a globally recognized example of participatory government where all persons, regardless of socioeconomic status, race, national origin, or religious and spiritual orientation, are actively involved. To be effective, all our citizens must be able to function at the high levels of intellectual, emotional, and social complexity required for meeting our beleaguered globe's economic, environmental, human, and political challenges.

Here is my personal take on some of those critical challenges. My international experiences traveling and consulting in fifty-eight countries on all the continents except Antarctica during the last forty years suggest that things are getting worse, not better. Many persons around the globe are experiencing life as more stressful and less meaningful than even during the cold war of the 1950s and 1960s. Certainly it is very much the case here in the United States. The ability of multinational corporations to move jobs to sources of cheap labor create unemployment problems where jobs leave and social disruption and dislocation in receiving countries. Our global communication systems let hackers in one location cause widespread havoc across national boundaries. A SARS outbreak in China becomes an international threat. Starvation and disease increase despite dramatic growth in food production capacity. International, intertribal, interethnic, interreligious conflicts flare up and seem immune to peaceful resolution. Politically driven disinformation and misinformation renders informed decision making and well-thought-through political activism almost impossible.

In the United States, we have a two-tier society in which the gap between rich and poor has grown dramatically. In 1980 the average CEO made forty-two times what an average hourly worker made. By 2005 the ratio was 262 to 1. Barack Obama, in his book *The Audacity of Hope* (2006), says, "Between 1971 and 2001, while the median wage and salary income of the average worker showed little or no gain, the income of the top hundredth of a percent went up almost 500 percent" (p. 192). We have recurrent violence and crime in our schools and colleges and on our streets, some driven by drugs, some apparently random expressions of rage and frustration. We have recurrent corruption in politics, corporations, and financial institutions. Each of you readers has your own list.

New Directions for Adult and Continuing Education • DOI: 10.1002/ace

Furthermore, powerfully driven by the events of September 11, 2001, issues concerning diverse religious and spiritual orientations have moved front and center in public forums and political decision making. Increasing our sophistication about these issues and framing the conversations to meet these challenges at the level of complexity they require, and developing the competence to pursue them, are critical if we are to sustain a civil, pluralistic, democracy.

Then, of course, there is the Internet. Andrew Keen's *Cult of the Amateur: How Today's Internet is Killing Our Culture* (2007) offers some penetrating perspectives. Keen's central argument is that the so-called democratization of the Internet is actually undermining reliable information and high-quality entertainment by replacing it with user-generated content that is sometimes unreliable and inane. Keen fears that it is not improving community, developing rich conversation, or promoting collaboration. The Internet reflects some of our best qualities: irreverence, vitality, excitement, and youthfulness. But it also reflects what Keen calls digital narcissism, the embrace of the self, a trend illustrated when *Time* magazine's person of the year for last year was "you." Keen does not believe that the key to citizenship is personal self-expression. For him, the key to citizenship is listening, and reading, and consuming high-quality information and entertainment. In Keen's view, the most corrosive element of today's Internet is the anonymity that creates an uncivil world because we don't reveal who we are. The Internet and the Web, with their interactive no-holds-barred culture, are key forces that call for a high level of intellectual and emotional competence anchored in solid information and well-thought-through perspectives.

There is also a critical change under way that requires all of us to become as competent as we can be in understanding, in talking with, and in working with people who differ widely in their political, religious, and spiritual orientations, in privilege and social class, in ethnicity and national origin. We are moving from "devolved communities" to "involved communities."

Social science research—and our own experiences—make it clear that we are social creatures. We mainly become who we are through relationships with others. We are socially constructed creations of community. For centuries, certainly since the beginning of recorded time, communities have been handed down to us. Typically those communities have been grounded in family, tribe, and place. They have been grounded in institutions and organizations created out of those contexts: neighborhoods, churches, schools, clubs, and local friendship networks. These communities were by and large stable and predictable. They were governed by inherited codes of conduct, some of which were spelled out in laws or other documents. But—as any of us who have grown up in a small New England village will recognize—the most important cultural norms have been informal, inexplicit, and unarticulated. The dynamics of power and the clashes of varied self-interests, while usually fairly widely known, were seldom publicly expressed. This

New Directions for Adult and Continuing Education • DOI: 10.1002/ace

kind of traditional community, this devolved community, does not exist for any external purpose or to achieve any particular goal. Its purpose is simply the nourishment and sustenance of its members. It meets deep human needs—for belonging and identity, for security and predictability. It meets the need to be accepted simply because of who we are, by the givens of our membership.

An involved community is not a given, passed down as part of our place and time; it is chosen. Depending on the roles we choose or accept, our participation does not offer predictability or comfort, but challenge. The time, energy, and emotion we invest give purpose and meaning to our lives. Active participation offers us a chance to create meaning for ourselves on the basis of our particular contributions to something larger than ourselves and our families.

Developmental Challenges and Perspectives

Times of crisis chill dissent in colleges and universities just as in the body politic. Just when our country can most benefit from the diverse perspectives that academe should provide, there are growing pressures to repress these views. Since the Middle Ages, colleges and universities have been a safe place to search for truth and to criticize injustice and oppression. We must protect our ability to educate students—including adult students, who are society's current voters, volunteers, and leaders—about our changing world, the clash of cultures, the great issues of world poverty and hunger, global warming and environmental degradation, alienation and apathy.

Education of this kind is not just teaching about these topics; this brand of education helps each individual integrate heart and mind, values and actions. Parker Palmer (2000) suggests the orientation we need:

> I must listen to my life and try to understand what it is truly about—quite apart from what I would like it to be about—or my life will never represent anything real in the world, no matter how earnest my intentions. . . . I must listen for the truths and values at the heart of my own identity, not the standards by which I *must* live—but the standards by which I cannot help but live if I am living my own life [pp. 3–6].

Listening for the truths and values at the heart of our own identities, clarifying the standards by which we will live our own lives, is a fundamental developmental challenge. The capacity to deal with the complexities of life with integrity for oneself and others lies at the core of every developmental theory. In Chapter One, Cecil Smith illustrates this capacity for complexity through the works of Kegan (1982, constructive-developmental), Gilligan (1982, moral development), and Erikson (1959, psychosocial development).

The stages and perspectives represented by these three theorists are congruent with three other theorists whose work I have drawn on consistently over the years. In Loevinger's stages of ego development (1976), an individual moves from impulsive and self-protective stages (Chickering's enflamed ideologists) through conformist (Moyers's lemmings) to a conscientious level characterized by self-defined standards and self-criticism (Palmer's truth speakers). Developmental movement then progresses to an autonomous stage, to an integrated level that cherishes human dignity, tolerates ambiguity, and struggles with the affective and cognitive complexities of our daily lives and public policies. This higher level of development is characterized in Perry's scheme (1970) of intellectual and ethical development as commitments in relativism—anchored in self-realized values subject to recurrent critical scrutiny. In *Women's Ways of Knowing* (Belenky, Clinchy, Goldberger, and Tarule, 1986/1996), the pinnacle of the five knowing perspectives—constructed knowing—represents knowledge as personally important, woven from reason and emotion, objective data and subjective experiences.

Perry's scheme and his associated dynamics recall to my mind Erich Fromm's *Escape from Freedom* (1941), and the "authoritarian personality" formulations of Adorno (1950). These social psychologists were trying to understand how the Germans, one of Europe's best educated and culturally sophisticated people, could have been led to support Hitler, engage in Kristallnacht, and tolerate the Holocaust. After being defeated in World War I, Germany suffered not only humiliation but also severe economic depression and uncertainty about the future. Fromm's theory is that under these conditions the populace "escaped from freedom" and gave themselves to the certainties of Aryan superiority espoused by Hitler and his collaborators. The authoritarian personality research posited a dynamic where, as a friend and colleague of mine put it, people "suck up and kick down." They needed scapegoats, and the Jews were handy targets (Adorno, 1950).

For me this sounds a lot like Perry's Dualism and his Escape and Retreat dynamics. Do we see similar responses and dynamics here in the United States in response to September 11? Does something like this lie behind some of the more extreme parts of the Homeland Security legislation, accompanied by unfettered surveillance and wiretapping?

The developmental progression of all of these theories is that individuals look for ways to transcend boundaries and resist oversimplification. They recognize that answers and solutions vary with the context in which they are raised and with the frame of reference of the people involved. My own candidates for indicators of higher-order functioning are knowledge pertinent to key social issues; intellectual competence; interpersonal competence; emotional intelligence; integrity; and a level of motivation that invests time, energy, and emotion in concerns larger than our own immediate self-interest.

From my view, having become increasingly socially conscious over the past fifty years, encouraging adult development—strengthening affective and cognitive complexity—has never been more important. Unfortunately, culturally and politically our society seems to be stuck at the self-protective, opportunistic, and conformist levels described by Loevinger (1976). Our typical ways of knowing are received (acquiescing to authority), subjective (limited to self), and procedural (governed by rationality) when we desperately need contextual, constructed ways of knowing (Belenky, Clinchy, Goldberger, and Tarule, 1986/1996). Penetrating and responding to the sound bites, lies and distortions, and ideological appeals that daily besiege us requires a high level of cognitive and affective complexity. Listening for the truths and values at the heart of our identities and clarifying the standards for our own lives becomes a daunting challenge—whether we are adult teachers or adult learners.

Practicalities for Personal Development

White (1981) noted that service to others offers some of the most developmentally powerful experiences we can have. There is now solid evidence that community based learning can contribute to the wide range of desirable outcomes that are consistent with a higher level of affective and cognitive complexity, as noted by the theorists that Cecil Smith and I have highlighted. Smith (Chapter One) identifies various studies that have reported significantly positive outcomes for students who participate in service learning. Another study worth noting is that of Sax and his colleagues (1999), who examined thirty-five student outcomes concerning civic responsibility, academic development, and life skill development:

> The most remarkable finding of this longitudinal study was that all 35 student outcomes measures were favorably influenced by service participation. . . . The largest differential change . . . occurred with the values "promoting racial understanding," "participating in community action programs," and "influencing social values." As a consequence of service participation . . . students became less inclined to feel that individuals have little power to change society [Sax, Astin, Korn, and Mahoney, 1999, p. 255].

Even though this prior research was carried out with typical college-age students, not with subsamples of adult learners, the findings certainly suggest powerful potentials. Other authors in this volume illustrate some of this potential. The findings also suggest the kind of useful research agenda that Smith articulates in Chapter One.

Given the potential of community based learning to stimulate adult learners' developmental growth—and the potential of developmentally mature adult learners to contribute their knowledge and skills in valuable ways—what do we educators and community partners need to understand

and do in service of the desired outcomes of engaged citizenship? Kolb's (1984) experiential learning theory of growth and development helps us understand why the desired outcomes occur. Many readers will be familiar with his cycles of concrete experience (CE), reflective observation (RO), abstract conceptualization (AC), and active experimentation (AE). Each of the major quadrants—divergence (CE and RO), assimilation (RO and AC), convergence (AC and AE), and accommodation (AE and CE)—represents a dialectical mode. Progress toward integrating any two or more of these dialectical modes brings about growth in affective, perceptual, symbolic, and behavioral complexity. This conceptual framework assists in explaining how service learning has powerful potentials to help adult learners become more complex in those four major domains. All of our educational practices need to include these four elements if developmental change is to occur.

For me, the most neglected element is reflection. Without it, there is little learning that lasts. Reflection is the process by which we metabolize our experiences so they nourish us. Experiential learning, especially service learning, dramatically enriches what we are asked to ingest. But without significant opportunities for collective and individual reflection—being force-fed and then asked to regurgitate—the resulting developmental nourishment is much less than it could be. In Chapter Seven, Fiddler and Marienau elevate reflective practices reported by the other authors and offer their own framework for reflection in community based learning that fosters meaningful learning. In an earlier, more extensive work, they present conceptual foundations, developmental outcomes, and strategies and exercises that help learners achieve the kind of outcomes critical for personal growth and for responsible citizenship (Taylor, Marienau, and Fiddler, 2000).

Pedagogical practices need to call for behaviors that are consistent with our desired outcomes and that generate learning that lasts: collaborative and problem-based learning, case studies, learning teams and research teams, socially responsible learning contracts, criterion-referenced evaluation. These pedagogical practices need to incorporate concrete experiences and reflection, applying and testing academic concepts, principles, and theories in real-life situations such as service learning. All these formal academic policies and practices need to be supported by faculty members who are psychologically, physically, and temporally accessible. Adult students, as well as traditional-age students, can express cynicism, self-involvement, and lack of multicultural sensitivity. Service learning is one avenue to help students engage in encounters with authenticity, empathy, and respect (Cone, Cooper, and Hollander, 2001).

In the institutional context, Boyer's "scholarship of teaching" and "scholarship of application" (1990) must be explicitly encouraged. Criteria and processes for faculty renewal, promotion, and tenure need to reward community contributions and civic engagement on and off campus. Institutional program evaluation needs to examine the degree to which varied interventions concerning curricula, pedagogical strategies, student-faculty relationships, peer interactions, experiential learning, and new governance arrangements actually improve civic learning and social responsibility among students, faculty, staff, and administrators. Each institution needs to determine what democratic collaboration means and how to practice it.

Conclusion

The basic premise here is that community based learning can be a powerful force for encouraging personal development and for strengthening democracy in our multicultural, globally interdependent, battered world. But to do so, it needs to pervade all our curricula, degree programs, learning contracts, and community partnerships. As Palmer (2000) reminds us, these changes will operate only on the surface if we professionals do not reclaim our own authenticity and sense of calling. That is a challenging agenda, but we must tackle it. It requires maintaining a steady fire. This is the posture we need.

References

Adorno, T. M. *The Authoritarian Personality: Studies in Prejudice.* New York: Harper, 1950.

Belenky, M. F., Clinchy, B. M., Goldberger, N. R., and Tarule, J. M. *Women's Ways of Knowing: The Development of Self, Mind, and Voice.* New York: Basic Books, 1986.

Boyer, E. L. *Scholarship Reconsidered: Priorities of the Professoriate.* San Francisco: Jossey-Bass, 1990.

Chickering, A. W., and Associates. *The Modern American College.* San Francisco: Jossey-Bass, 1981.

Cone, R., Cooper, D. D., and Hollander, E. L. "Voting and Beyond: Engaging Students in our Representative Democracy." *About Campus,* 2001, 6(1), pp. 2–8.

Erikson, E. *Identity and the Life Cycle.* New York: International Universities Press, 1959.

Fromm, E. *Escape from Freedom.* New York: Holt, Rinehart & Winston, 1941.

Gilligan, C. *In a Different Voice: Psychological Theory and Women's Development.* Cambridge, Mass.: Harvard University Press, 1982.

Keen, A. *The Cult of the Amateur: How Today's Internet Is Killing Our Culture.* New York: Currency, 2007.

Kegan, R. *The Evolving Self: Problem and Process in Human Development.* Cambridge, Mass.: Harvard University Press, 1982.

Kolb, D. *Experiential Learning: Experience as the Source of Learning and Development.* Upper Saddle River, N.J.: Prentice Hall, 1984.

Loevinger, J. *Ego Development: Conceptions and Theories.* San Francisco: Jossey-Bass, 1976.

Moyers, B. "Which America Will We Be Now?" *Nation,* Nov. 19, 2001, pp. 11–13.

Obama, B. *The Audacity of Hope.* New York: Crown, 2006.

Palmer, P. *Let Your Life Speak.* San Francisco: Jossey-Bass, 2000.

Perry, W. G. *Forms of Intellectual and Ethical Development in the College Years: A Scheme.* Austin, Tex.: Holt, Rinehart & Winston, 1970.

Sax, L. J., Astin, A. W., Korn, W. S., and Mahoney, K. M. *The American Freshman: National Norms for Fall 1999.* Los Angeles: UCLA Higher Education Research Institute, 1999.

Taylor, K., Marienau, C., and Fiddler, M. *Developing Adult Learners*: Strategies for Teachers and Trainers. San Francisco: Jossey-Bass, 2000.

White, R. W. "Humanitarian Concern." In A. W. Chickering and Associates (ed.), *The Modern American College*. San Francisco: Jossey-Bass, 1981.

ARTHUR W. CHICKERING is special assistant to the president of Goddard College, Plainfield, Vermont. He is the author of several books and numerous articles concerning college impacts on student development.

New Directions for Adult and Continuing Education • DOI: 10.1002/ace

9

Adults' engagement in community based learning offers new perspectives on persistent issues, future research questions, and priorities for action—leading toward deepened commitment to civic engagement.

Maintaining a Steady Fire: Sustaining Adults' Commitment to Community Based Learning

Susan C. Reed, Catherine Marienau

Twenty-five years ago, Art Chickering challenged us to "maintain a steady fire" of commitment, words that are repeated in full in his chapter in this volume. He cautions us that commitment is not a raging fire that burns out when youthful energy encounters adult responsibilities and realism, or is doused by critique and resistance. Adult commitment, he implies, is fueled by creativity and reflective thought, by critical analysis and tough-minded testing. Similarly, Daloz, Keen, Keen, and Parks (1996) identified adults who are "committed to the common good" as those who "held strong convictions yet were not fanatical, who had a clear focus yet were not blind to other perspectives, who held a large and inclusive vision yet were not simply idealists, and who, while working on behalf of particular constituencies, understood them to be working on behalf of the whole of life" (p. 6). Chickering's words, those of the authors of *Common Fire,* and the work of the authors in this volume inspire us to consider how community based learning can contribute to developing adults who learn from active engagement in their communities, are able to appreciate the complexity and diversity of our society, and are willing to respond with integrity to social issues in their own way, according to their own values and standards, throughout their lives.

In consideration of this aim, this chapter addresses three forward-looking questions. The first is simply, *In what ways can community based learning promote lives of commitment in adults?* The second is, *How can we*

NEW DIRECTIONS FOR ADULT AND CONTINUING EDUCATION, no. 118, Summer 2008 © 2008 Wiley Periodicals, Inc.
Published online in Wiley InterScience (www.interscience.wiley.com) • DOI: 10.1002/ace.299

(faculty and the staff of community organizations) design community based learning experiences, as well as reflection on them, to enhance adult commitment? Third, *What can institutions of higher education do to support faculty as well as community organization staff in their efforts to engage adults in community based learning?* For this analysis, we draw on many of the facets of adult commitment found by Daloz and colleagues in their study of adults who maintain engagement throughout their lives.

As we explore these questions, we keep before us the concept of the "involved community" that Chickering envisions, one that we choose and build over the course of adulthood with the roles that we adopt and the challenges to which we rise. Daloz, Keen, Keen, and Parks (1996) describe the "new commons" of the twenty-first century as "global in scope, diverse in character and dauntingly complex" (p. 3), which requires adults to engage with people from different cultures and recognize our interdependency. Community based learning as an ideal seems well equipped to offer adults the skills and relationships needed to develop such communities, but we caution ourselves and the reader to remain critical rather than idealistic, to test our assumptions rather than jump on a bandwagon, and to engage in the tough-minded testing that cool passion requires.

Promoting Lives of Commitment

How can community based learning promote lives of commitment in adults?

The complexity of modern life challenges adults, more than ever, to understand other perspectives, tolerate ambiguity, and recognize the relationship of context to knowing. Both Smith (Chapter One) and Chickering (Chapter Eight) are looking to community based learning to promote the highest levels of development in adults, such as an ethic of care for Smith, or constructed knowing for Chickering. Whether, and how, community based learning can help develop such skills is a researchable question that could be studied over time. Particularly relevant to citizenship is the role generativity (the developmental stage of adult development at which we experience the desire to nurture future generations) plays in adult motivation to engage in community based learning and the extent to which such work satisfies a developmental need in adult learners (see Smith, Chapter One). Snyder and Clary (2003) used the Loyola Generativity scale to examine the role that generativity plays in adult motivation to volunteer, and they found a correlation. Their research design could be adapted to the study of adult participation in community based learning courses. It would also be possible to discover whether such courses help develop generativity in adults (McDermott, 2007). Smith (Chapter One) cautions that such development is gradual and not easily studied within academic calendars, although he shares a strategy for examining "microdevelopment" that has been used in similar research.

New Directions for Adult and Continuing Education • DOI: 10.1002/ace

Besides personal development, community based learning may offer the opportunity for a "constructive engagement with otherness" (Daloz, Keen, Keen, and Parks, 1996), an encounter with significantly different others who one comes to recognize have struggled with some aspect of life in a similar way (p. 54). In their study of committed adults, Daloz and colleagues found that such an experience was a common thread. However, they warn that encounters with otherness can simply reinforce preconceptions about groups without leading to a "sympathetic identification" that can be transformative (p. 67). Their concern is reflected in the service learning literature, where despite the many positive outcomes that have been associated with those who participate in service learning there remains concern about whether unequal relationships between students and community residents is fostered with this methodology.

Service, some argue, can reinforce perceptions of helpless community residents and encourage a professional approach to problem solving that sees people in the community as needy while members of the university are problem solvers (Eby, 1998). Speck (2001) argues that this professional relationship to community residents perpetuates "the status distinction between those who help and those who need help" (p. 9). In fact, it may even reinforce feelings of powerlessness among recipients of service (Nadler, 2002) by focusing on "fixing" the individual rather than addressing aspects of the community that foster inequality and injustice (Clary and Snyder, 2002). When one must work interdependently with someone else, one is forced to see beyond the stereotype that one brings to the relationship; on the other hand, if one perceives the other person to be relatively powerless, then one feels no need to question the stereotype (Schwarz, 1998).

For these reasons, Speck (2001) calls for a "civic approach" to community based learning rather than a "philanthropic approach." Instead of offering services to others, according to this view educators must help students see themselves as active participants in a democratic culture by "teaching our students to explicitly identify and critique their own interests and to make these interests the basis for their community work" (Morton and Enos, 2002, p. 97). There is evidence that the skills needed for adults to address personal concerns in the public sphere can be taught through community based learning, as Kirlin (2002) explains, although she notes that Perry and Katula's review (2001) of the literature found that service learning was more effective in promoting cognitive understanding of citizenship skills than in advancing active citizenship behavior among adults. Patrick (2000) argues that community based learning courses could develop citizenship skills by engaging in certain activities: "interacting with other citizens to promote personal and common interests, monitoring public events and issues, deliberating about public policy issues, influencing policy decisions on public issues and implementing policy decisions on public issues" (Kirlin, 2002, p. 5). Such activities seem well designed to prepare adults for engagement in their own community. This opportunity can enable

New Directions for Adult and Continuing Education • DOI: 10.1002/ace

adults to develop a network with civic associations that can lead to a life-time of engagement. But they may be less likely, at least in the short run, to cross the borders of race and class than adults engaged in a project with members of another community.

Richter-Hauk and Arias (Chapter Three) designed their community based learning course with the objective of developing professional values and offering culturally appropriate services. One of the outcomes seemed to center on "cultural consciousness," defined by Daloz, Keen, Keen, and Parks (1996) as "the recognition that we dwell in cultures—patterns of human behavior shaped by a particular community or population over time" (p. 116). When Julie Arias advised her students to talk to the children of the Mexican families at her community center in Ohio, she was hoping to foster relationships that would afford insight into another culture from the inside, through the lens of children who tend to be both observant and open. Their students articulated a beginning understanding of cultural differences and an awareness of their own assumptions about which country is "better." The students also sought to offer information in return about their own culture. What worries proponents of such interaction is whether, in the short time frame of a class, the depth of such interactions leads to cultural consciousness or "simply a superficial 'tolerance' by which one glibly confers value on another culture without engaging it" (Daloz, Keen, Keen, and Parks, 1996, p. 116). At best, such experiences are a first step toward recognition of one's limited understanding and a desire to learn more.

Mündel and Schugurensky (Chapter Five) challenge those of us in higher education to consider what children and adults are learning from their interactions at such community centers as well. While those of us engaged in community based learning at colleges and universities are studying adult development among students, these authors are focusing their attention on adult learning in the community. They are asking the parallel question, Do the efforts of adults volunteering in their communities lead to their growth and to lives of commitment? A volunteer in their study was able to articulate the difference between respect and tolerance in her growing understanding of those whose sexual orientation was different from hers. In this case, the authors attributed these insights to opportunities for conversation with other volunteers or community organization staff. With adult students or volunteers, Dewey's maxim cited frequently by adult educators and service learning scholars holds: community based experiences do not result in learning or adult development without reflection.

Designing Events and Reflection

How can we design community based learning "events," as well as reflection on them, to enhance adult commitment?

Whether an adult's goal is to gain a better understanding of our complex and diverse environment or to actively engage in addressing the social issues facing us, learning from community based projects can be designed to offer "the first step" (Daloz, Keen, Keen, and Parks, 1996). Without intentional reflection on a community based event (whether a volunteer experience or one designed in the classroom), learning at the level we're seeking is less likely to occur (Fiddler and Marienau, Chapter Seven). By the same token, not just any experience in the community will offer the substance that leads to transformation in an adult's perspective.

Scholars of community based learning (Eyler and Giles, 1999) as well as adult volunteering (Clary and Snyder, 2002) find a strong association between demonstrated benefit of community based learning and the participants' perceptions that their work is meaningful to the community. Eyler and Giles (1999) found that students demonstrate greater personal growth if they participate in a community based project that they perceive to be contributing to the larger goals of a community organization or nonprofit. Research on volunteerism among adults has found that long-term involvement is heavily influenced by the quality of their placement in the community, particularly in terms of the volunteers' perception of how they and others were treated by the organization (Penner, 2002) as well as their opinion that their work is meaningful to the community (Clary and Snyder, 2002).

For a community based project initiated by a college or university to truly engage adults, faculty and community staff must work closely together around objectives that are determined collaboratively as modeled by Richter-Hauk and Arias (Chapter Three). Unless each partner takes responsibility for both the practical aspects of a community based activity and reflection on it, adults are likely to report the perception that their activities are not meaningful to the community, and that they did not feel engaged with the mission of the organization, as did some students in Largent and Horinek's study of their first year (Chapter Four). In such collaboration, the community partner considers how student volunteers can best serve their organization's mission. The project must be manageable for their staff, appropriate for the level of students' skills, and hopeful of accomplishing something within a relatively short period of time (a quarter or a semester). Ideally, as Largent and Horinek show, community partners recognize the skills and prior experience that adults bring to their community based work and engage in conversation or intentional reflection in the community about students' observations and responses. Such active engagement with students on the part of community partners asks a lot for little or no compensation by the university, in most cases; but studies have found interest among community partners in playing this educational role (Worrill, 2007).

Bringle and Hatcher (2002) apply the principles of a healthy relationship to the partnership of faculty and community organizations to emphasize the importance of interdependency between both parties. Faculty often approach community organizations from the standpoint of the expert bringing resources to the community rather than as equals sharing mutual resources (Holland, 1997). For a collaboration to function effectively for a faculty member and a community partner, both parties must feel that their input to the effort is proportional to the outcome. This interdependency is fostered by frequent and diverse forms of communication between faculty and staff collaborator; community organizations must have reason to believe that not only are their interests considered by faculty but decisions and actions are influenced by those interests (Holland, 1997).

This ideal is difficult to achieve. Faculty often rely on service learning centers on campus to establish and monitor students' experiences in the community (Holland, 1997), in part because of the trade-offs they make in allocating their time (Marienau and Reed, Chapter Six). Students sometimes return to their classes for reflection on their experiences at these sites that faculty have never visited. The community partner, in such cases, does not understand the learning objectives of the course and is not engaged in reflection with students about their experiences.

An interdependent relationship between a faculty member and community partner could result in a long-term community based project where adult students work collaboratively with, rather than for, their peers in the community. Unlike the increasingly out-of-date image of the traditional student who comes to the community to attend a college or university and then leaves, adult students are likely to be members of the community. Therefore we have the opportunity to design projects that link adults with others who share their aspirations for practical action (Daloz, Keen, Keen, and Parks, 1996) in a reciprocal trade of knowledge or skills. Given that community residents bring assets as much as needs to any community based project (Kretzmann, McKnight, and Sheehan, 1997), partners could identify those assets and design an exchange rather than a service project (such as Spanish speakers and English speakers trading language instruction; Sanchez and Moore, 2005).

Such projects need not end with the term, or even graduation. Adult students often welcome the entrée to community engagement that a community based learning project presents them, given the difficulty of connecting to volunteer or civic action opportunities that they might otherwise never hear about (Reed and Marienau, 2006). Lifelong engagement with others can develop two habits that Daloz, Keen, Keen, and Parks (1996) found in their study of committed adults: the habit of "*dialogue,* understanding that meaning is constructed through an ongoing interaction between oneself and others," and the habit of "interpersonal *perspective-taking,* the ability to see through the eyes and respond to the feelings and concerns of the other" (p. 108).

Faculty and staff who accomplish the design of quality events that challenge adults' assumptions, build equitable relationships, and promote meaningful social change have laid the groundwork for learning through reflection. The parallel challenge is to design and facilitate discussion that draws out aspects of an event that catches adults' attention, identify related

beliefs and assumptions, and offer to adults theories and ideas of others that
might deepen their experience, with the potential of transforming their
understanding of themselves and their world (see Fiddler and Marienau,
Chapter Seven). Daloz, Keen, Keen, and Parks (1996) found that sustaining lives of commitment required adults to develop three additional habits
of thought: the habit of "critical, *systemic* thought, the capacity to identify
parts and the connections among them as coherent patterns, and to reflect
evaluatively on them"; the habit of "*dialectical* thought, the ability to recognize and work effectively with contradictions by resisting closure . . ."；
and the habit of "*holistic* thought, the ability to intuit life as an intercon-
nected whole . . ." (p. 108). Mündel and Schugurensky (Chapter Five) show
how dialogue with co-workers through board debriefings and conferences
resulted in volunteers' understanding of the systemic roots of strain on nonprofits trying to deliver public services, as well as an understanding of the
dialectic between local and national efforts for housing reform. How can
reflection on community based learning be designed to achieve such habits
of thought that will enable adults to act constructively within an increasingly diverse and complex world?

According to Eby (1998), this type of systemic analysis is seldom
achieved in the service learning classroom. Students who do service learning often enter the community from outside. This reinforces the idea that
the community itself is deficient and needs outside resources to work at its
problems. By defining needs as deficiencies, students are able to separate
themselves from the problems they encounter. They fail to see that often the
same social structures that work well for them create the needs in the communities in which they do service learning. By focusing on individual need
and individualized service, students miss the systemic nature of social life.

In fact, reflection on community based learning often reveals students'
interpersonal perspective that attributes much of human experience to mis-
fortune or personal choice. Rubrics have been developed that assist faculty
and students in articulating learning that indicates higher-order thinking
skills (Ash, Clayton, and Atkinson, 2005). Fiddler and Marienau (Chapter
Seven) caution the facilitator of reflection to guide students in this analysis
rather than feed it to them, because guidance seems more likely to develop
the habit of paying attention to events and beginning to recognize the connections and patterns between events that make up complex systems and
social structures.

Developing habits of systemic and dialectical thought that is linked to
activism has been the objective of popular education for many years (Freire,
1972). Adult educators have drawn on these principles to offer learning
opportunities that are not necessarily classroom-based. Their scholarship as
well as studies of informal learning (see Mündel and Schugurensky, Chapter Five; Stein, 2002) present strategies for reflective practice through dialogue that community organizations could use to promote learning among

volunteers, as could models such as the CELI programs discussed by Holland and Robinson (Chapter Two).

The authors in this volume show how much planning is involved in designing community based projects, and in facilitating reflection on events that occur in the community. They emphasize the importance of both to the promotion of learning for students as well as volunteers. The potential for community based learning as a means of developing a lifelong commitment to learning through community engagement is substantial. Yet these expectations cannot be met solely through the tireless efforts of faculty and community organization staff committed to this methodology. What's needed is institutional support and reinforcement that builds on their labor, supplying a structure that enables others to perpetuate it.

Supporting Faculty and Organization Staff

What can institutions of higher education do to support faculty as well as community organization staff in their efforts to engage adults in community based learning?

The rising number of adult and other nontraditional students offers an opportunity to institutions of higher education to build on students' networks in the community, thereby strengthening relationships with community organization staff, expanding learning opportunities, and encouraging ongoing civic engagement among students. Holland and Robinson (Chapter Two) show how so many facets of adults' lives, including the workplace, are noticing the benefit to adult development when adults experience the satisfaction of working for the public good. The authors mention that some of these endeavors recognize the importance of learning to development, while others do not. Linking these efforts with colleges and universities to a greater extent could allow faculty to lend their expertise to promoting learning among volunteers in co-reflection with students (Eyler and Giles, 1999).

Where students are community residents, colleges and universities have the chance to develop ongoing partnerships with community based institutions, agencies, and organizations such that goals are established collaboratively that go beyond the class project to longer-term endeavors. Adults who make their first step toward civic engagement in the classroom would have opportunities to continue their involvement; faculty could work across disciplines to build scholarship around these efforts. At the same time, adults who are civically engaged when they enter the college or university could organize their learning around their community experiences, perhaps gaining credit for prior learning (see Marienau and Reed, Chapter Six). Institutions that successfully develop such relationships with community partners tend to involve community leaders in planning and evaluation and demonstrate a commitment to redesigning programs to reflect community interests (Holland, 1997).

Before dedicating resources to developing community based learning for adults, institutions of higher education will ask two questions: Will adult students sign up for community-based learning courses? Will the changes recommended to enhance adult learning benefit students of all ages? Empirical data regarding adults' interest in or development from community based learning are scant, because age as a variable is rarely included in service learning research. We hope this issue presents enough evidence of the distinctive characteristics of adult learners (see Marienau and Reed, Chapter Six; Largent and Horinek, Chapter Four), the developmental potential of community based learning with adults (see Smith, Chapter One; Richter-Hauk and Arias, Chapter Three; and Chickering, Chapter Eight), and of the nontraditional student becoming increasingly traditional (Holland and Robinson, Chapter Two) to interest scholars in focusing attention on these learners. Holland and Robinson (Chapter Two) report two studies in which students who work actually participate in greater numbers, suggesting that adults appreciate the practical learning opportunities afforded by community based learning. Largent and Horinek (Chapter Four) found that although satisfaction among adult service learners was lower in their first year, changes in the design of their program increased satisfaction overall, indicating that adults will demand meaningful projects and interaction as well as recognition of prior learning, but that students of all ages will profit.

With a growing trend toward online learning to serve the working adult student, a few creative practitioners are developing techniques for monitoring partnerships from a distance and stimulating thoughtful reflection over the Internet (Strait and Sauer, 2004; Rapp, 2007). Adults can benefit from the opportunity to establish projects in their own community, drawing on their own networks, and develop relationships that are integrated into their lives (see Marienau and Reed, Chapter Six). Strait and Sauer (2004) advise faculty and university staff to make sure that there are clear means of communication with each community partner so that they may be fully integrated into the educational and evaluative process. Facilitating reflection that solicits adults' own interpretations and offers connections to the ideas of others may be even more challenging online than in the classroom. This could become a significant area of collaboration between scholars of online learning and community based learning in the future.

Conclusion

As adults, we have a desire to give back to the communities that have supported and nurtured us, and we find our own ways to do so. Community based learning is but one mechanism for making connections that enable us to satisfy the aspiration to address the many problems of concern. It is a methodology that can be employed in the classroom, the workplace, volunteer sites, retirement centers—wherever adults are working with others to improve their communities and are reflecting on those experiences. With reflection may come personal growth and commitment to a life of community engagement.

The challenge of sustaining that commitment in the face of the many demands on our time and attention has been the focus of this chapter. Daloz, Keen, Keen, and Parks (1996) have four pieces of advice for those adults hoping to maintain that steady fire: take the first step, link with others who share your aspirations for practical action, take care of yourself, and spend time with young people (p. 217). These simple words of wisdom could also help those of us hoping to sustain a commitment to community based learning.

To those of us in the scholarly community: let's begin to engage in (qualitative or quantitative) research on community based learning that includes age as a variable so that we can identify best practices in supporting adults in their quest for civic engagement. Those in the service learning community will benefit from scholarship in adult learning, and vice versa. In addition, those working within the broader field of adult education where students are not seeking a degree, along with the field of public education, will hopefully join this conversation to enhance our knowledge and practice.

As educators, we too benefit from the opportunity to cross borders of race and class within our cities and between our institutions and communities. The relationships we build will foster our own growth and development as well as that of our students. Let's build reflection into any program that links adults with community, whether in the workplace, community organization, or classroom; and engage regularly in dialogue that promotes learning. In this process, let adults lead the way, even if it means listening and responding to their complaints. Adults bring to community based learning their networks, their skills and knowledge, and often a burning desire to address the needs that Chickering and others feel are so urgent.

References

Ash, S. L., Clayton, P. H., and Atkinson, M. "Integrating Reflection and Assessment to Capture and Improve Student Learning." *Michigan Journal for Community Service-Learning*, 2005, 11(2), 49–59.

Bringle, R. G., and Hatcher, J. A. "Campus-Community Partnerships: The Terms of Engagement." *Journal of Social Issues*, 2002, 58(3), 503–516.

Clary, E. G., and Snyder, M. "Community Involvement: Opportunities and Challenges in Socializing Adults to Participate in Society." *Journal of Social Issues*, 2002, 58(3), 581–591.

Daloz, L. A. P., Keen, C. H., Keen, J. P., and Parks, S. D. *Common Fire: Lives of Commitment in a Complex World.* Boston: Beacon Press, 1996.

Eby, J. W. Why Service-Learning is Bad. 1998. http://www.messiah.edu/external_programs/agape/servicelearning/articles/wrongsvc.pdf.

Eyler, J., and Giles, D. *Where's the Learning in Service-Learning?* San Francisco: Jossey-Bass, 1999.

Freire, P. *Pedagogy of the Oppressed.* London: Penguin, 1972.

Holland, B. "Analyzing Institutional Commitment to Service: A Model of Key Organizational Factors." *Michigan Journal of Community Service Learning*, Fall 1997, 30–41.

New Directions for Adult and Continuing Education • DOI: 10.1002/ace

Kirlin, M. "Civic Skill Building: The Missing Component in Service Programs?" *PS: Political Science and Politics,* 2002, *35*(3), 571–575.

Kretzmann, J., McKnight, J., and Sheehan, G., with Green, M., and Puntenney, D. *A Guide to Capacity Inventories: Mobilizing the Community Skills of Local Residents.* Evanston, Ill.: Institute for Policy Research, Northwestern University, 1997.

McDermott, D. "Service Learning: Focus on Generativity and Care." *Academic Exchange Quarterly,* 2007, *11*(3), 129–134.

Morton, K., and Enos, S. "Building Deeper Civic Relationships and New and Improved Citizens." *Journal of Public Affairs,* 2002, Supplemental Issue 1: Civic Engagement and Higher Education, 83–102.

Nadler, A. "Intergroup Helping Relations as Power Relations: Maintaining a Challenging Social Dominance Between Groups Through Helping." *Journal of Social Issues,* 2002, *58*(3), 487–502.

Patrick, J. J. "Introduction to Education for Civic Engagement in Democracy." In S. Mann and J. J. Patrick (eds.), *Education for Civic Engagement in Democracy: Service Learning and Other Promising Practices.* Bloomington: Indiana University ERIC Clearinghouse for Social Studies/Social Science Education, 2000.

Penner, L. A. "Dispositional and Organizational Influences on Sustained Volunteerism: An Interactionist Perspective." *Journal of Social Issues,* 2002, *58*(3), 467–477.

Perry, J., and Katula, M. C. "Does Service-Learning Affect Citizenship?" *Administration and Society,* 2001, *33*, 330–333.

Rapp, A. "Engaging with Community: Creating Online Service Learning Courses for Adult Students." Futures of Adult Higher Education, 27th National Conference of the Adult Higher Education Alliance, Dayton, Ohio, Oct. 2007.

Reed, S., and Marienau, C. *Linking Adults with Community: A Study of Motivation, Reflection and Problem Solving Among Adult Service Learners.* Presented to International Conference on Service and Community Based Learning; Portland, Ore., Oct. 15, 2006.

Sanchez, B., and Moore, A. *A Qualitative Evaluation of the Bringing It Home Service Learning Program.* A Report to the Steans Center for Community Service Learning, DePaul University, 2005.

Schwarz, N. "Warmer and More Social: Recent Developments in Cognitive Social Psychology." *Annual Review of Sociology,* 1998, *24*, 239–264.

Snyder, M., and Clary, E. G. "Volunteerism and the Generative Society." In E. de St. Aubin, D. McAdams, and T.-C. Kim (eds.), *The Generative Society: Caring for Future Generations.* Washington, D.C.: American Psychological Association, 2003.

Speck, B. W. *Why Service-Learning?* New Directions for Higher Education, no. 114. San Francisco: Jossey-Bass, 2001.

Stein, D. "Creating Local Knowledge Through Learning in Community: A Case Study." In D. Stein and S. Imel (eds.), *Adult Learning in Community.* New Directions for Adult and Continuing Education, no. 95. San Francisco: Jossey-Bass, 2002.

Strait, J., and Sauer, T. "Constructing Experiential Learning for Online Courses: The Birth of E-Service." *Educause Quarterly,* 2004, *27*(1). http://connect.educause.edu/library/abstract/ConstructingExperien/39848?time=1194202086.

Worrill, L. "Asking the Community: A Case Study of Community Partner Perspectives." *Michigan Journal of Community Service Learning,* 2007, *14*(1), 5–17.

SUSAN C. REED *is associate professor in the School for New Learning, DePaul University. Her research and teaching has focused on disparity in access to health care, as well as community based learning with adults.*

CATHERINE MARIENAU *is professor and faculty mentor in the School for New Learning, DePaul University.*

INDEX

YOUR **free** ISSUE OF

NATIONAL CIVIC REVIEW
is now available online. Go to
www.interscience.wiley.com/journal/NCR

WILEY
InterScience®
DISCOVER SOMETHING GREAT

National Civic Review

◉ Get Sample Copy
◉ Recommend to Your Librarian
◉ Save journal to My Profile
◉ Set E-Mail Alert
✉ Email this page
🖨 Print this page

Special Issue
on Performance
Measurement
and Reporting

In this Issue:

- Public Employees as Partners in Performance: Lessons From the Field *by Brooke A. Myhre*
- Starting Performance Measurement From Outside Government in Worcester *by Roberta Schaefer*
- Current Approaches to Citizen Involvement in Performance Measurement and Questions They Raise *by Anne Spray Kinney*
- Bridging the Divide Between Community Indicators and Government Performance Measurement *by Ted Greenwood*

WILEY
Publishers Since 1807

Wiley and the Wiley logo are trademarks of John Wiley & Sons, Inc.

Complete online access for your institution

Register for complimentary online access to *Journal of Leadership Studies* today!

OPT-IN TO COMPLIMENTARY ACCESS:

- Institutions can opt to receive complimentary online access to *Journal of Leadership Studies* through 2008!
- When your complimentary online access ends, there is no obligation to subscribe.
- If you choose to continue with complete online access, pricing will be based on the overall demand during the term of the complimentary access, and on the size and type of subscribing institution (academic, corporate, hospital, government).

REGISTER TODAY AT:

www.interscience.wiley.com/newjournals

The opt-in model is designed to establish fair pricing and to encourage usage and uptake. The period of complimentary access will enable institutions to ascertain usage and demand for a new journal before signing up for a paid subscription. In addition to complimentary online access, institutions and companies may request one complimentary print subscription.

Opt-in access is only available to qualifying institutional customers.